D0065756

Housing Policy and the State

SOCIOLOGY, POLITICS AND CITIES

Editor: JAMES SIMMIE

PUBLISHED

John Lambert, Chris Paris and Bob Blackaby: HOUSING POLICY AND
THE STATE

FORTHCOMING

Manuel Castells: CITY, CLASS AND POWER
Manuel Castells and Francis Godard: MONOPOLVILLE
Nicholas Deakin: THE FAILURE OF POSITIVE DISCRIMINATION
Patrick Dunleavy: THE POLITICS OF COLLECTIVE CONSUMPTION
Brian Elliot and David McCrone: THE MODERN CITY
Alan Hooper: MARXIST VIEWS OF URBAN SOCIOLOGY
Valdo Pons and Ray Francis: SLUMS AND SHANTY TOWNS
James Simmie: POWER, PLANNING AND THE DISTRIBUTION OF
PROPERTY

Housing Policy and the State

Allocation, Access and Control

JOHN LAMBERT
CHRIS PARIS
BOB BLACKABY

© John Lambert, Chris Paris and Bob Blackaby 1978

All rights reserved. No part of this publication may be reproduced or transmitted, in any form or by any means, without permission.

First published 1978 by
THE MACMILLAN PRESS LTD
London and Basingstoke
Associated companies in Delhi Dublin
Hong Kong Johannesburg Lagos Melbourne
New York Singapore and Tokyo

Printed in Hong Kong

British Library Cataloguing in Publication Data

Lambert, John
  Housing policy and the state. – (Sociology, politics and cities).
  1. Housing – England – Birmingham   2. Housing – Great Britain.
  I. Title   II. Paris, Chris   III. Blackaby, Bob   IV. Series
  301.5'4'0942496   HD7334.B/

  ISBN 0–333–23223–2
  ISBN 0–333–23224–0   Pbk

This book is sold subject to the standard conditions of the Net Book Agreement.

The paperback edition of this book is sold subject to the condition that it shall not, by way of trade or otherwise, be lent, resold, hired out, or otherwise circulated without the publisher's prior consent, in any form of binding or cover other than that in which it is published and without a similar condition including this condition being imposed on the subsequent purchaser.

Contents

Editor's Preface

The eruption of conflicts in cities on both sides of the Atlantic during the 1960s has lead to dissatisfaction with the urban paradigms of the 1920s and new scholarly attempts to explain the relationships between social and spatial structures. The series 'Sociology, Politics and Cities' is designed to provide a platform for these debates.

The series focuses on alternative theoretical formulations of the social and political factors forming and developing cities. Emphasis is laid not only on single-disciplinary approaches to such understanding but also on attempts to build transdisciplinary ways of theorising about urban settlements. These contain elements of history and economics as well as sociology and politics.

Two types of book are being published in the series: small works containing reviews of existing theoretical formulations or excursions into new ones; and substantial works usually based on original research and combining both theory and evidence in the analysis of various aspects of cities.

The small books contain work on various schools of urban sociology and politics ranging from those based on Weber to those based on Marx. The large books contain analyses of many aspects of cities ranging from slums to ecology and from power to policy.

In addition to the theoretical and empirical analysis of cities the series also focuses on the problems of and prospects for intervention in the development of settlements. In many cases this engages a concern for public policy although examples of such private initiatives as shanty towns are also examined. Policies such as the urban programme, housing, race relations and planning are included in this vein.

Housing Policy and the State: Allocation, Access and Control illustrates a

number of important characteristics of the British contribution to the
renaissance of urban sociology and politics.

In the first place it remarks on the growing dissatisfaction with the old
paradigms for the study of cities based on the works of the important
Chicago School. This leads to the original adoption of an action frame
of reference for the study of the relationships between actors in the
housing problems found in the inner areas of cities like Birmingham.
The rise of the Paris School during the course of the research is also
reflected in criticisms and modifications of the original theoretical
starting points. Secondly, the book provides an example of one
alternative to the traditional British empirical approach in sociological
analysis. Instead of the familiar survey a participatory action–research'
method was employed. The insights into the meaning of situations and
problems from the point of view of the actors concerned are discovered
as a result of the adoption of this technique. Finally, the book illustrates
the growing sense of disenchantment and futility felt by consumers of
some of the outputs of the welfare state. Having had a generation of
experience with the operation of such policies as comprehensive
redevelopment in the name of planning, many people now question the
relevance and ability of, for example, local planning bureaucracies to
deliver goods on the ground that match the castles in the air of local and
central government promises.

In total the book brings readers to a point in the mid-1970s where the
social and economic problems of the poorer inhabitants of cities are
relatively well documented. It poses the question now facing scholars
and policy-makers alike of how best to explain these problems in terms
of theory and what to substitute for previous failed policies and
inadequate forms of local government. These are questions which will
be taken up by other books in the series.

London 1977   JAMES SIMMIE

Acknowledgements

This book derives from research undertaken in Birmingham between 1970 and 1974. The methods adopted mean that the number of contributors who should be acknowledged is especially large. Most of the informants were unaware that they were helping a small research team based at the Centre for Urban and Regional Studies to fulfil a project funded by the Social Science Research Council. Broadly speaking, these anonymous and unwitting contributors were of two sorts: the residents of the neighbourhoods in which we worked; and various employees in departments of Birmingham City Council. Our debt to each group is considerable. We hope that some of our work with the groups and organisations trying to represent the interests of 'ordinary' people in the neighbourhoods in some part repays a debt. Regarding the 'managers', we would not like a careless reader to construe the book as an attack on the incompetence of local officials and councillors. To do so would be to 'blame the victim': our concern is that the potential and limitation of local government be recognised and that the efforts of those who labour in large 'faceless' offices with scarce resources and contradictory guidelines be more clearly appreciated. Perhaps if we point out that one of us has now joined their ranks without any sense of contradiction, given our 'findings' reported here, our point will be made.

Some of our aiders and abettors were not anonymous and we would like to put on record our debt to them. During the research John Lambert was employed by the Sparkbrook Association, which allowed him to maintain a part-time appointment to perform his research duties. We are grateful to the Association's Council and Executive for allowing this. The Balsall Health Association, the Lane Neighbourhood Centre, the Midland Area Improvement Housing Association, and

WELD were other organisations which provided the research–action opportunities recorded here. Dick Empson, Margaret Selby and Chris Wadhams bore the brunt of our involvements without flinching most of the time – they will know how much we derived from their work. Special acknowledgement is due to Robert Jenkinson and the Residents' Association of which he was secretary, for his contribution to the research and for the mass of material made available to us.

Joint architect of the whole project was Camilla Lambert, whose full-time involvement was foreshortened by the demands of motherhood. Thereafter hers was a more diffuse but no less considerable influence on the outcome. At the Centre for Urban and Regional Studies, the initial project was supported by Professor J. B. Cullingworth. After his leaving the Centre, Professor Gordon Cherry provided valuable support and encouragement. The Social Science Research Council provided funds for a pilot project – 'Ethnic Choice and Preference in Housing' – and for the main project – 'Neighbourhood Associations and Housing Opportunities'.

Secretaries and typists too numerous to mention suffered the tasks of turning too many pages of impossible handwriting into legible typescripts of various kinds culminating in the preparation of this book: we are grateful for the facilities provided by University College Cardiff and the City of Birmingham Polytechnic as well as the Centre for Urban and Regional Studies.

It will be apparent that our debt to the above merits more than the conventional acknowledgement; and by the same token the conventional disclaimer that none should be held responsible for the views expressed in this text but ourselves can hardly be overstressed.

Chapter 1
On Theory and Urban Sociology

This book is structured around close and careful scrutiny of events and issues in four neighbourhoods in the inner city areas of Birmingham between 1971 and 1974. We believe that what occurred is of relevance for a general understanding of urban problems and policies in Britain in the 1970s and that similar stories could be told about many other cities in modern Britain. Of course, there are special features about Birmingham, its size and history, which need to be grasped to make full sense of what was happening and to these we have drawn the reader's attention in the text. But it is in the hope that the specifics of time and place can aid more general understanding that we have constructed this book around four case studies. They are the evidence for our more general statements, assertions and judgements.

However, we have not simply recounted a story that we happened to observe: we have selected certain themes and instances; we had prior assumptions about what was important to study; our methods provided access to some informants but not to others; thus, in that sense, ours is a biased account.

There are of course innumerable vantage points from which to study and report on the myriad fascinations of city life. Let us, straight away then, try and make explicit our vantage point and prior assumptions – the theoretical orientation or perspective which has shaped our accounts of housing and planning issues in Birmingham.

In Search of an 'Urban' Sociology

This study has sought first of all to be a contribution to urban sociology; but the current status of urban sociology is such that there is no common or widely accepted definition of what constitutes a distinctly *urban* sociology. In a country like Britain, is not everywhere, or at least every*one*, 'urban' now? Most people live in or near major cities; our culture is available to virtually the whole population at the turn of a switch on the television or radio, or through the daily media. Indeed, as differences between ways of life ('country' *versus* 'town') become blurred, 'urban' can simply come to mean a relative and arbitrary geographical category, or a particular stage in social development towards advanced 'urban/industrial society' (Reissman, 1964).

For many years 'urban sociology' was synonymous with an approach to the study of urban phenomena influenced by the human-ecology school founded in Chicago in the early part of the twentieth century. Between 1850 and 1920 Chicago was transformed from a small lakeside port to a bustling metropolis as wave after wave of European migrants arrived there to settle in the New World. It was an exciting and stimulating place rapidly expanding and changing – the ideal laboratory, perhaps, in which to study the relationships between urban growth and social change. For the sociologists and anthropologists at the University of Chicago the city was their workshop, and they were fascinated by the social organisation of urban space, the relationships between ethnic groups and the persistence of problem areas characterised by crime and deviance. Their theoretical perspective began with the Darwinian concept of the 'web of life' and extended the analysis of ecological relations identified by Darwin between living organisms (plants and animals) to the study of social relations between human groups (Park, 1925).

They stressed the processes of urban change, the balance between different organisms and areas and the influence of size, density and heterogeneity on urban relationships (Wirth, 1938). This sociology generated an amazing variety of fascinating detailed studies of many aspects of urban living – continued to the present day with more and more elaborate systems of mapping and describing the social areas of cities. However, as Ruth Glass observed, this school of urban sociology increasingly lost contact both with the mainstream of sociological thought and with any theoretical context. In Britain, despite early 'pragmatic' urban sociology of the 'Booth tradition', there was scant interest among sociologists in the urban dimension of their studies and contributions to the field came from the fields of human geography, town planning and anthropology (Glass, 1955).

It was not until the mid- to late 1960s that there was any shift in interest among sociologists. Why this should be so is not really within the scope of this chapter but there is little doubt that the 'crisis' of the cities in the United States and the political tensions in Britain relating to the presence of a predominantly urban 'immigrant' minority influenced the development. *Race, Community and Conflict* (Rex and Moore, 1967), commissioned by the Institute of Race Relations in 1963 and published in 1967, was the first study for many years that applied a specifically sociological perspective *and* a critique of the Chicago school. For Rex, Burgess's theory of urban growth (Burgess, 1925) was, significantly, a starting point (Rex, 1968). For many earlier studies it was the finishing point as well.

For Burgess the 'core' of the city was the central business district, and the forces which distributed urban populations in concentric rings about that core were those of the market. However, the Chicago sociologists, and other ecological studies, did not really analyse the forces of competition and conflict deriving from the nature of that market, 'urbanism' being identified uncritically with the specific cultural system of *laissez-faire* capitalism. It was precisely these forces which Rex and Moore were interested in examining, but they were also concerned to study the influence of bureaucratic non-market processes on individuals' life chances.

In their particular study they were concerned with the way in which local councils influenced the social distribution of housing opportunities:

> Houses in a modern city are not allocated simply by a process of competition in the market, a substantial part of housebuilding is today carried out by local governments. It seems to us that participation in this public estate is a considerable prize in a society where housing is a scarce resource and that such a public estate can bring into being a group whose 'market situation' in the housing market is an especially privileged one. This brings us to a point which appears to be central to the sociology of the city. Put simply, there is a class struggle over the use of houses and this class struggle is the

central process of the city as a social unit . . . men in the same labour
market may come to have differential degrees of access to housing
(Rex and Moore, 1967, p. 273).

For Rex and Moore, then, the object of urban sociology became the
task of revealing the underlying pattern of social relations in order to
explain, rather than merely describe, the nature of urban development.
Their notion of 'housing class' developed from this interest, for it was
not enough to refer, as Burgess had, to an abstract process of
'competition' for housing. Rather, 'What is needed is an account in
terms of the action frame of reference which explains particular kinds of
land-use and building use in terms of the action-orientation of typical
residents' (Rex, 1968, p. 212).

Thus 'the class struggle over the use of houses' was separable from
industrially defined class relations, and 'housing classes' were structured
by both economic *and* bureaucratic/political factors. In this way Rex
argued it was possible to 'make sense of the process underlying Burgess's
theory of urban zones'. The theory of housing classes 'tells us something
of the potential basis of conflict and must further specify the ways in
which those with a common "market situation" organise or fail to
organise to take action in pursuit of their interests' (Rex, 1968, p. 211).

The notion of housing classes and its concern for the relations
between urban populations and the administrative and bureaucratic
organisation of local government was developed by R. E. Pahl, whose
route to an interest in urban sociology lay not through race and the
inner city but through an interest in the sociology of suburban and
exurban housing development in London's commuter fringe (Pahl,
1965, 1968). In a provocative and influential essay he argued that a
'truly urban sociology' was to be located in the study of the distribution
of various 'urban resources', principally housing, but also transport,
education and other facilities, and to show to whom, by whom and in
what ways access to these facilities is granted. The interplay between
social and spatial constraints upon such opportunities of access was the
focus of his redirected urban sociology, and the crucial actors for study
were the 'managers or controllers of the urban system' (Pahl, 1969).

Our Birmingham study started out to develop this urban sociology in
relation to housing issues in Birmingham's inner city. It was one among
a number of studies in this vein (see Norman, 1975). As our work
progressed, however, we began to modify and reject some of its central
and underlying assumptions. This was not a case of initial hypotheses

requiring modification under the influence of empirical data, although it was the case that much of what we observed and wanted to explain did not rest comfortably within our adopted paradigm. We were influenced by a somewhat different ciritique of conventional urban sociology which developed in France after 1968 and which was becoming available to English scholars in the form of partial, mimeographed translations from 1972 onwards. In 1973 *Social Justice in the City* (Harvey, 1973) was published; this invited a major rethink on urban issues through the application of Marxist theory. Ralph Miliband's *The State in Capitalist Society* was another book whose paperback version (Miliband, 1973) arrived in timely fashion to assist our understanding of the role of the state. However, before enlarging upon these influences, it may be useful to draw attention to certain features of the Rex/Pahl formula for urban sociology in relation to which these other studies and theorisations are in contrast.

Critical Features in the Ideas of 'Housing Class' and 'Urban Managerialism'

Rex's conception of 'housing class' derives from a view of class relations and social stratification developed by Max Weber and one which is an immensely powerful tradition in sociological thought. Also, the methodological prerequisite of the 'action frame of reference', which Rex acknowledges, owes its origins to Weberian thought, and stands in opposition to that school of sociological theorising known as structural-functionalism (Silverman, 1970, pp. 126–46).

In this system of ideas it is claimed that the natural drift of social organisation is towards balance and integration of its many complex parts. The Chicago school and its stress on ecological *balance*, albeit deriving from competition, on *natural* areas, and on universalistic traits discernable in urban development, is a variant of structuralist thought. Man in this scheme tends to be presented as subject to forces contained in institutional or systemic arrangements which have the power to constrain and control. The 'action frame of reference' belongs to an opposing sociology concerned to avoid the *reification* contained in so much structuralist conceptualisation in terms of systems and institutions. With the 'action frame of reference' a sociological explanation is one which puts 'man as actor' on the centre of the stage and seeks to explain institutions and systems in terms of the men and women who make and sustain them.

Within the 'action frame of reference' the concern is with how actors define their situation, with their beliefs and understanding of their social world, and with the action taken based on that understanding, with the capacity of actors to change institutions rather than be controlled by them.

In structural-functionalism, although conflicts and disagreements are common, the natural drift of social organisation is towards a consensus and towards co-operation; indeed, it is the function of institutions to limit the scope of conflict and to enlarge the area of normative agreement.

Within the action frame of reference, conflicts, disagreements and clashes of interests are continuous, constant and real, given the variety of interests, beliefs and ideas which people have and given the variety of interactions and relationships. If structural-functionalism is the sociology of order – the social system is a sociological model or analogy for an ordered world – the action frame of reference depicts a world where interest groups collide, collude and cohere in the control of institutions, where privilege and status are negotiated, where, in short, power becomes the crucial variable.

Institutional arrangements, then, can be studied to reveal, and to be explained as, the outcomes of struggles between conflicting and competing social groups. For both Rex and Pahl the style and purpose of a truly urban sociology are fairly clear. This can be seen in the notion of 'housing class'. In Rex's original formulation he argues that, following Weber, class relations are to be sought not just in the sphere of work and production but in any market situation, and in this sense to talk of differential relations to the 'means of housing' identifies separate housing classes. Rex identified seven such classes – seven distinct housing situations arranged in a hierarchy of esteem reflecting the exercise of differential power in the making and maintaining of those situations (Rex, 1968, p. 215).

It is central to the Rex scheme that the *present* housing situation, indicating a market relationship, includes a *power* variable. This, as Haddon cogently observes, confuses *use* with disposal: 'The use of housing is an index of achieved life chances not a cause. The ability to dispose of property or skill in the market depends on the existence and strength of a market' (Haddon, 1970). The means of *access* to housing is crucial for any notion of housing class in the Weberian sense and this is what is missing in the Rex formulation.

Pahl has offered a reformulation which avoids categorisation in terms of the present housing position and gives primacy to access by making the possession of capital the crucial differentiating factor. His suggested housing classes are (Pahl, 1976, p. 245):

(1) large property owners, public or private;
(2) smaller landlords (e.g. charitable trusts);
(3a) owners of capital sufficient to own their own houses and owning;
(3b) owners of capital sufficient to own their own homes and renting; and
(4) those who *must* rent.

However, this formulation is extremely confusing, particularly the references to public and private landlords and to charitable trusts. Indeed, if what is being sought is a categorisation of classes of the population in terms of their means of access to housing as a specific part of consumption (i.e a home in which to live), categories 1 and 2 are redundant, for they merely specify a means of obtaining capital for consumption of housing while indicating forms of control over other people's access to rented housing (categories 3b and 4). Categories 1 and 2 are likely to be owners of capital sufficient to own their own houses and owning, although some may choose to rent. So essentially it is a model in which money (savings or access to a loan) is crucial. By 'sufficient' Pahl presumably means those who have insufficient capital to be outright owners but can borrow and whose interest is in appreciation of their limited capital investment and the maintenance of relative low-cost housing of a desired quality.

This model, as Pahl himself acknowledges, cannot cope with the large public-rented sector, whose rules deny eligibility for everyone who must rent while providing opportunities for some of those who could own but who choose to rent instead. In Rex's formulation, too, although the existence of the council-house sector is acknowledged and given great significance, it remains unanalysed – the existence of something analogous to a market situation is presumed. However, in the public sector there would seem to be little sense of a *market* in which a person has something to *dispose*. Few of the bureaucratic rules of allocation are rights enforceable by an individual or even by some collective exercise of power. Power and control rest within a particular and localised aspect of the political machinery. Moreover, it would seem to be clear that beyond the public sector the existence of 'planning' as a part of state enterprise influences every aspect of the housing market in defining zones for varieties of land use, in its limitations on urban growth, in terms of its preferred densities and in its capacity to define whole areas of cities as safe or uncertain in terms of housing investment.

This, of course, is why Pahl's emphasis on the role of urban managers is so important. His original formulation included the recommendation that urban managers (and the list was extremely broad and not restricted to local-authority managers) should be considered as 'the independent variable' (Pahl, 1969, p. 215). We took this to mean that 'the managers' were an important source of influence over how resources were distributed locally, but not that they were in some way autonomous allocators who were completely independent of central state and market forces (Paris and Blackaby, 1973). In Pahl's revised version of his 'urban managerialist' thesis, some of this confusion is cleared up when he reminds us that 'urban managers' are, after all, only 'middle dogs'; they may play a socially mediating role but their full autonomy cannot ever be assumed (Pahl, 1975, p. 268). However, the nature of this mediation is both crucial and problematical. Underlying both the Rex and Pahl formulations of a truly urban sociology are assumptions about the nature of political power and of the state.

If we look to the Rex and Moore study, although there is a fairly extensive political commentary, the interests and activities of the city council are treated as in some way balancing and arbitrating the competing demands of different power groups. Control over council-house allocation is referred to as 'prize', and there are depictions of city officials managing contradictory elements of policy – as in the treatment of landlords of multi-occupied property as a pariah group in the formal and legal terms of housing and public health law yet serving an indispensable function for housing provision at times of acute shortage. Pahl has developed his conceptualisation of the state in terms of 'corporatism', one in which 'managerialism' both in industry and in state and local-authority provision of essential goods and services plays an important part.

Such views are consistent with the Weberian sociology of class relations and with the action frame of reference. It is a formulation of politics and state power which has been the dominant perspective in political sociology for some time – that of democratic pluralism. In our next section we will examine this conception further. We may conclude this section on the developing ideas of an urban sociology by noting that while Rex and Pahl's new direction for urban sociology fetched it clear from the aridities of the Chicago school, it was also a critique which located the study of urban development firmly within the dominant mode of academic thought in the Anglo-Saxon tradition.

Our empirical work in Birmingham started with a concern to study relations between 'the managers' and 'the managed', focused on the allocation of housing in four discrete neighbourhoods. As we will describe later, the 'action frame of reference' required us to forgo conventional techniques and methods of research and adopt a particular strategy of work in the chosen neighbourhoods.

However, as our work proceeded, it was in relation to the underlying assumptions about the state and managerialism in our adopted paradigm that we experienced most difficulty. Our case studies will explore this more fully and our concluding chapter is devoted to the problem. The difficulty led us to the rather different new direction for urban sociology provided by French scholars adopting a specifically Marxist viewpoint. It may be useful at this stage to preface an outline of this work with some comments on differing theories of the state.

The State in Capitalist Society

'More than ever before men now live in the shadow of the State.' Thus Ralph Miliband starts his analysis of the Western system of power (Miliband, 1973, p. 3). Yet he notes that 'the State itself, as a subject of political study, has long been very unfashionable'. A vast literature exists on government, public administration, parties, voting behaviour, etc. which touches on the nature and role of the state but which leaves the institution itself hardly analysed at all. The absence of study, Miliband notes, does not of course mean the absence of a theory and he goes on to argue that the dominant form of theory of the state in political sociology explains why there is so little analysis. Most political science and sociology starts, he says,

with the assumption that power in Western societies is competitive, fragmented and diffused; everybody directly or through organised groups has some power and nobody has or can have too much of it. . . . As a result the argument goes, no government, acting on behalf of the State can fail, in the not very long run, to respond to the wishes and demands of competing interests. In the end, everybody, including those at the end of the queue, gets served. There are, in Western societies, no predominant classes, interests or groups. There are only competing blocks of interests whose competition, which is sanctioned and guaranteed by the State itself, ensures that power is diffused or balanced and that no particular interest is able to weigh too heavily upon the State (Miliband, 1973, pp. 4–5).

Miliband quotes two eminent sociological figures who give expression to these assumptions:

the fundamental political problems of the industrial revolution have been solved; the workers have achieved industrial and political citizenship; the conservatives have accepted the welfare state; and the democratic left has recognized that an increase in overall State power carried with it more dangers to freedom than solutions for economic problems (Lipset, 1963).

Through industrialized development under democratic auspices the most important legitimately-to-be-expected aspirations of the 'working class' have in fact been realized (Parsons, 1964).

The pluralist conception of the state asserts that the managerial revolution in industry, allied to social-democratic forms of representative government, has transformed capitalism to render notions of class struggle and class conflict obsolete. The sphere of production and man's relation to the means of production are not dominant; the levels of wages, the sphere of consumption, socialised provision of certain common goods and facilities, these are the fundamental determinants of social relations in the contemporary Western world. The essential nature of state machinery is conceived in terms of the role of *arbiter* among competing interests to organise the maximisation of interest satisfaction.

It should be apparent how the formulations of Rex and Pahl are broadly consistent with this Weberian view of social organisation.

Pahl's most explicit formulation derives not from his work on urban sociology but from his study, with Winkler, of business managers (Pahl and Winkler, 1974a). In 'The New Corporatism' Pahl and Winkler (1974b) have sketched a model of government they believe will be explicit by the 1980s and whose main components can be discerned in present trends. Corporatism is extensive state control without nationalisation, state ownership, and is the direction of privately owned business towards four goals – order, unity, nationalism and 'success' – through 'imposing   intense   state   control   in   all   major   areas   of   private economic activity'. The authors dismiss as 'fantasies which provide a measure of liberal desperation' suggestions that this corporatism will be constructed on the basis of democratic decision and consent; but they are ambivalent or obscure about the process, merely acknowledging that for some it will still be capitalism while for others it will be a means of 'building socialism'. For our purpose, however, it is significant that the state is represented as the arbiter of competing or more truly contradictory interests and will itself impose its own will and purpose. How different groups would fare under corporatism is considered and a kind of prediction is offered that only working-class activity could face a major change in the pattern of future events.

Such a conceptualisation begs, it would seem, all the questions of the pluralist model of political power of which it is a variant, while implying a Marxist analysis in places. Who or what precisely is 'the state', by what means of management will it be sustained, and in whose interests, both relatively and absolutely, can it be said to function? All these are doubts and issues which parallel those concerning the assumptions about the state which rest with Pahl's managerialism thesis.

It should also be apparent that the 'action frame of reference' is a methodological approach consistent with this democratic pluralism, both in its revealing of multiple definitions of situations, meanings, attitudes and values, and in its concern for variant styles of life of which beliefs are a part.

Miliband's analysis, on the other hand, seeks to demonstrate that the growth of the state has not transformed the essential class nature of society. He points out that in those Western countries typified by 'advanced' capitalism and social-democratic forms of government, 'by far the largest part of economic activity is still dominated by private ownership and enterprise . . . whatever ingenious euphemism may be invented for them, these are still, in all essentials and despite the transformations which they have undergone, authentically capitalist societies' (Miliband, 1973, p. 12).

The role of the state is to manage – particularly in the sphere of consumption – the interests of private ownership. It is the contemporary vehicle for the maintenance of social order. Given that the state is now the prime provider for collective needs and provides the administration for solutions to 'urban problems', struggles between working-class and ruling-class interests will not be restricted to the work-place but will occur wherever class interests are in conflict. We should expect therefore to observe struggles both *against* the state and *through* the state machinery, as working- or subordinate-class interests attempt to transform it into a more just vehicle for the provision of their collective needs – and as those who currently control and benefit from the state machinery resist further erosion of their privilege and seek to minimise the 'ransom', they must pay for remaining in control.

In this perspective, any study of 'urban managers' retains value and interest. But what needs to be avoided is the study of managers as some kind of autonomous group whose effects are to be measured in relation to their claims. Such a study might present the ideas, values, beliefs and definitions of planners as something distinctive and having a direct influence on events. In short such a study would accept as given the claims for autonomy for serving the community or the public interest, which are not uncommon in planning circles. Instead the subject matter of urban managerialism and its characteristic supporting beliefs and world views – planners' ideology – should be studied to demonstrate the real interests and purposes of state action. Since the state, both central and local, can act either to reinforce or change existing patterns of resource distribution and since policies and practices of an urban administration do produce differential effects on various groups, evidence for the state's interests and methods of control can be ascertained.

Miliband devotes two long chapters to the 'process of legitimation' whereby the form and content of class domination are mitigated and assented to by 'the majority' (Miliband, 1973, pp. 161–236). Our empirical study has focused in some detail on the importance to be attached to ideas, attitudes and beliefs in the maintenance of social order. What we have termed managerial *style* is instrumental in sustaining the deference, acceptance and consent towards objectively unsatisfactory policies and practices by typical residents in our study neighbourhoods.

The concept of *ideology* has a particular place in the Marxist theory of the state. Miliband acknowledges that since the state is the main agent of the mitigation of class domination in Western countries, it has been able to present itself with some plausibility as the servant of society. There is a definition of ideology which states: 'when a particular definition of reality comes to be attached to a concrete power interest, it may be called ideology' (Berger and Luckmann, 1967). Frequently the concept of ideology is used to refer to any more or less comprehensive system of ideas with which different groups manage their world, and so it is possible to speak of 'planners' ideology (see, for instance, Davies,

1972). However, in a Marxist analysis like that of Miliband the whole point of ideology is its obscurantist purpose – its masking of something *real*. Different ideologies are not particular versions or competing definitions of reality or the truth; all ideologies are sets of assumptions which oppose what is true or real.

We should notice that in Miliband's analysis part of the process of legitimation of the role of the state in class domination rests with the dominant academic conceptualisation of the state and of power. When we turn to the work of the French urban sociologists, this concern with, and definition of, ideology is central.

The New Urban Sociology

For Castells, the leading theoretician of the new urban sociology utilising a specifically Marxist viewpoint, as for Rex and Pahl, the Chicago sociology provided a point of departure. But as Pickvance points out, to see Castells's critique as similar to those of Glass or Pahl would be 'basically to misunderstand their author's purpose' (Pickvance, 1976, p. 3). Castells's initial purpose was to distinguish between theory and ideology in urban sociology (Castells, 1969), and to contribute towards laying the foundations for a sociological analysis of urban politics (Castells, 1970).

The critical question which Castells posed was whether urban sociology was scientific or ideological and, if the latter, whether a scientific urban sociology was possible or whether the whole enterprise was inherently ideological and therefore to be rejected. Castells's use of terms was quite specific and followed from a particular version or 'reading' of Marxism – that of Althusser. In this, *scientific* knowledge is 'distinguished by its possession of a specific theoretical object', i.e. 'science' studies a real object which has concrete existence in the real world by means of theoretical objects, particular concepts relating to the real. Thus 'a science which has neither a specific theoretical object nor a specific real object does not exist as a science'. That does not mean it will not have institutional existence and practitioners and devotees, but such will be ideology not science and will produce 'not knowledge but misknowledge' (Castells, 1969, p. 60).

When Castells reviews the work of the Chicago ecologists, he is concerned with the concepts utilised to further study of the real object – the city. The central concept 'urbanism', he avers, describes 'the cultural expression of capitalist industrialisation, the emergence of

a market economy and the process of rationalisation of modern
society (Castells, 1968, p. 38). It is a concept based on two related
theories:

(1) that modern (i.e. capitalist/industrial) societies have a distinctive
cultural system which is the end-point of the process of development of
the human species; and

(2) that this system is the product of a particular ecological form,
namely the city (Castells, 1969, p. 66).

In relation to the former Castells argues that 'for urbanism to be the
specific theoretical object of urban sociology rather than merely the
culture of liberal capitalist society, it would be necessary to identify it
with modernity and assume that all societies are moving towards it as
they develop, despite secondary differences, e.g. those concerning their
economic systems' (Castells, 1969, p. 68). He goes on to suggest that
within the theory of urbanism, as in (1) above, there is an implicit stress
on the process of integration to the distinctive cultural system, and 'a
discipline which restricts itself to the study of social integration to a
particular culture – in this case the culture produced by capitalist
industrialisation – gives itself very limited scope for theoretical development (Castells, 1969, p. 68). In this way Castells develops a
critique of the functionalist assumptions of the Chicago theorists. In
relation to the second theory, he is more dismissive: 'The idea that a
form of social organisation (urbanism) could be produced by ecological
changes represents too impoverished a vision of sociological theory to be
seriously defended' (Castells, 1969, p. 68). Essentially he sees the
production of urbanism as arising from an increase in the size,
heterogeneity and density of the typical form of settlement to be not so
much wrong as simplistic: 'Characteristics such as these must not be
neglected, but rather must be incorporated into the technico-social
structure underlying the organisation of any society' (Castells, 1969,
p. 68).

He concludes his critique thus: 'Urbanism is not a concept. It is a
myth in the strictest sense, since it recounts, ideologically, the history of
mankind. An urban sociology founded on urbanism is an ideology of
modernity ethnocentrically identified with the crystallisation of the
social forms of liberal capitalism' (Castells, 1969, p. 70).

Does this mean that for Castells there can be no urban sociology? In
some ways his conception of the kind of study required to explicate

'urban problems' is so different that to use the same term seems inappropriate. As Castells argues: 'New theoretical formulations are necessary in order to explain the growing importance of "urban problems" in the management of society to specify their scope and to bring out the social mechanisms underlying them.'

He asserts:

Traditionally, work in urban sociology has been located within the problematic of social integration, as is to be expected given the nature of the demand to which it is a response, a demand closely linked to a reformist paternalism seeking to wipe away the misdeeds of capitalist industrialisation in the field of collective consumption.

Now in advanced capitalism urban problems are increasingly the subject of political debate and are the focal point for new forms of class struggle. The analytical tools forged by urban sociology are thus not only instruments of accommodation to the system as they always have been, but, as research tools, are completely incapable of accounting for the essential characteristics of the problems posed by social practice (Castells, 1970, p. 147).

For Castells the real as against the ideological object of an urban sociology must be the process of capital accumulation, which is central to the capitalist mode of production. The adjective 'urban', freed from the ideological connotations of 'urbanism' or 'urban culture', relates to an agglomeration whose function relative to consumption is similar to the function of the firm in relation to production: the boundaries of the agglomeration are set by the processes of consumption.

The relationship between production and consumption in a market economy is closely integrated. The concentration of production units – firms, sections of industry, in short *capital* has led to a concomitant concentration of population into relatively small spatial areas. But this process contains many contradictions, manifest in both nineteenth-century Britain and France and contemporary Third World cities – squalor, disease, disorganisation – all fundamentally structured around the basic contradiction between the *planned* nature of capitalist production within individual enterprises and the unplanned competitive relations between capitalist producers (see Lojkine, 1972). The history of urban development under capitalism is thus a history of attempts to resolve this contradiction, of the growing importance of the state (central and local) in the management of 'urban problems'. The development of capitalism has involved both the accumulation and concentration of capital, but those affected by this development and concentration have not merely responded passively to these changes in their work and domestic milieux. As Castells has argued, the development of capitalism has been accompanied by

> the development of the democratic and workers movements and their conquest of political liberties and social guarantees as far as standard of living is concerned . . . historically defined social claims for a series of basic rights – housing, education, health facilities, culture, leisure pursuits – whose provision is becoming more and more collective and interdependent. This body of collective needs increases continually whereas at the same time it is generally an unprofitable sector for capitalist investment. Collective consumption (housing, etc.) thus becomes at one end and the same time *an indispensable functional element of capitalist economy* (due to the concentration of the work force), a permanent subject of demands from the work force, *and an unprofitable sector of capitalist economy* (Castells, 1973).

Urban problems are therefore related to the provision of goods and services and their consumption within a spatial unit – the agglomeration, the city. Indeed the unit is defined by its consumption processes, and this, it should be noted, is *collective* consumption, i.e. the goods and services are characteristically for the collective population of the unit – homes, schools, leisure complexes, health centres, etc. – and not like other products intended for individual consumption. *Problems* relate both to collective consumption and to the organising and functioning of the unit as a whole in so far as changes in the unit also have effects on the consumption processes in question. The role of the state in urban problems is as prime provider of items for collective consumption and as administrator and manager of conflicts which arise or could arise given the nature of this provision.

Here, then, are the real and theoretical objects for a truly urban sociology: the sociology of space and the sociology of collective consumption. The former relates to the 'determination of the organisation, in relation to space, of individuals and groups, work places, functions and activities' (Castells, 1969, p. 77). Historically, Castells notes the growing importance of the political system in the management of space through the means of urban planning and the 'town planning system'. The sociology of collective consumption entails study of the relationships and processes whereby resources to facilitate the operations of production in a given space – specifically the resources to facilitate the reproduction of labour for production – are maintained. The provision of housing, education, leisure facilities, health facilities, transport, etc. for the needs of the population with the urban agglomeration comprise collective consumption. Again, the historical development of the role of the state in this provision is to be noted, but since the provision is a part of state enterprise such provision becomes a matter of *political* significance, and the study of *urban social movements* whereby groups seek to influence the process of provision becomes of primary sociological concern (Castells, 1970).

Castells stresses that these two analytical fields – urban planning and urban social movements – are indissolubly linked, for if the former focuses on *structures* and the latter on *practices* then 'structures are only articulated practices and practices only relations between relations defined by certain combinations of structural elements' (Castells, 1970, p. 149).

In what way, it might be asked, does this 'new' urban sociology differ from that developed by the English critics of the Chicago School – Glass, Rex and Pahl? It should be apparent that both sets of critics take sociology beyond the revelations of detailed ethnography, while recognising that the variety and detail are what need to be explained. Both sets of critics focus on the central importance of the *management* of the urban system; but the differences emerge in the treatment of the *political*, in the schema and terminology used to explain phenomena. The most succinct expression of differences is that provided by Pickvance in his article 'On the Study of Urban Social Movements' (Pickvance, 1975a).In that he points out, in explicit fashion, the different sort of study that Castells and his colleagues are involved in and how the differences derive crucially from the specifically Marxist theoretical base: the Marxist assumption about social change deriving from *class struggle* and the view that if 'the State expresses, in the last instance and through the necessary mediations, the overall interests of the dominant classes, then urban planning cannot be an instrument of social change, but only one of domination, integration and regulation of contradictions' (Castells, 1973, p. 18). In a later paper Pickvance (Pickvance, 1975b) has also used Rex's concept of 'housing class' in a critique of the French structuralist position. For Rex, and for those within the Weberian tradition, different classes emerge around different *markets* – hence pluralistic forms of government mediate the multiplicity of interests that arise. For Castells the economic instance is ultimately determinate and the process of capitalist accumulation and the contradictions which follow lead to a variety of forms of class domination. In short the crucial distinguishing factor concerns the role attributed to the state and its various apparatuses.

Conclusions

In this chapter we have attempted to describe and explain the ideas and influences which guided our study of housing and planning issues in Birmingham and which help to explain how we have selected events and occasions to include in our account and why we have stressed some elements and not others. In our final chapter we will seek to relate the findings and conclusions from our empirical project to the theoretical questions and issues raised here. It may be useful to provide a summary of our position:

(1) Our starting point was the prevailing inadequacy of urban sociology in Britain. The legacy of the Chicago ecologists, allied to policy and administrative concerns – the much publicised 'urban crisis' – tended to generate a host of detailed local studies or problems as defined by government or to aid techniques being developed by planners. What constituted a distinctly *urban* sociology was far from clear.

(2) The work of Rex and Pahl suggested, however, how a distinctly urban focus might develop. From Rex and the concept of 'housing classes', our interest became focused on how groups differentially placed in relation to the means of housing organise or fail to organise in pursuit of their interests. The view of the city as an arena for class struggles was made explicit. From Pahl derives the crucial determining focus for urban sociology on the managers and controllers of scarce urban resources and on the relations between the managers and the managed.

(3) Problematical in the urban sociology of Rex and Pahl, however, is the nature of the markets giving rise to classes and of the autonomy of the managers and controllers from the central economic processes of society. Both writers adopt a Weberian view of class, status and power and of the mediations carried out by government.

(4) However, the 'action frame of reference' which informs this Weberian urban sociology provides a valuable corrective to the

positivistic structural-functionalism of social-system sociology.

(5) A different kind of structuralism is apparent in the urban sociology of Manuel Castells and the school which shares a similar perspective. However, it too is a sociology interested in the processes of control and management but one which is based on a class analysis of social change and of the role of the state in advanced capitalism.

(6) Accordingly, in our empirical study of the provision of housing as a resource for collective consumption, we were concerned to examine relations between the controllers and managers of housing, to explore the saliency of the 'housing class' construct, to examine the interests and the mediations undertaken by the managers and to discuss the potentiality for, and the constraints upon, the emergence of urban social movements through the detailed consideration of aspects of the practices of the local urban planning system.

Here, then, were elements in our theoretical perspective which have informed our study and writing. Our empirical report is in the form of four neighbourhood case studies, we need to preface those, however, with an explanation of our method and a sketch of the housing question in Birmingham during the time when our work was undertaken.

Chapter 2

From Theory to Method

In the previous chapter we outlined a general theoretical perspective which could inform a number of actual empirical investigations. We should again stress the point that in common with most research practice, rather than the formal models of many textbooks, the interplay between theory and practice in our study was continuous; what we have summarised is our developing perspective during the process of research. That process contained empirical elements which influenced and were influenced by the readings and ideas that we have described.

There are, then, no simple formulae which adequately cover the transition from theory to method. It is important, however, to locate our empirical enquiry within the general perspective outlined, and to acknowledge how its origins and antecedents limit its scope and character within that perspective. It should perhaps be stressed that our enquiry is not an empirical application of the new urban sociology we have outlined. That much will become apparent to anyone familiar with the empirical products of the French urban sociology and with Castells's framework for an empirical study of urban social movements. Our interest in that sociology is more with its central concerns rather than its methods.

Within the general perspective, however, we would suggest that there are three interrelated themes which suggest separate but interlinked levels of study requiring distinctive methodological approaches. An empirical urban sociology embraces this broad range of concerns and methods.

The first of these three themes is the *development of capitalism* as a whole, which in the context of urban development concerns the financial provision for elements of collective consumption and their link with the dominant modes of capitalist enterprise. The second theme is the element of *social control*, whereby the interests and privileges of the dominant class are secured *and* whereby a stable work-force is ensured to maintain the dominant mode of production. Here the ideologies and practices of intermediary managers of state institutions and of the legal and administrative framework for collective consumption become targets for investigation. The third theme is the *reaction* – opposition or compliance – of the working-class towards the development of capital and the forms of social control which accompany it. Here the locus of study is the urban population and their organised groups (see Harloe, 1975, pp. 9–14).

Our empirical work concentrated on the latter two themes or levels, especially the third. We have sought to shed some light on the social relations which exist between urban populations and the local urban managers (or gatekeepers to the scarce urban resources which comprise collective consumption).

The focus on housing as the resource whose provision we examine derives from a previous research enquiry concerned with the sociology of race relations and the policy issue of the dispersal of coloured immigrants from the inner city. In many respects the narrow resource focus and the specific inner-city locus of research is a limitation in relation to any ideal empirical enquiry of 'urban management', but given the research antecedents and the practicalities of research funding and organisation it could hardly have been otherwise. However, the previous study was primarily concerned with the development of method, so if the theoretical starting point outlined above was something which emerged during the course of the study, aided and abetted by the work of Pahl and Rex in this country, of Castells and his associates and of Harvey in the United States, the attempt at a somewhat novel methodology was a prior undertaking.

The Limitations of 'Conventional' Research

At the risk of setting up something of a straw man, it may be helpful to sketch how a study using conventional methods might have approached our subject matter. Thereafter we can explain how our method of enquiry differed.

In the selected neighbourhoods – and, as in our study, selection presumes some foreknowledge of issues and events – the researcher would be expected to have spent some time meeting some key informants, local leaders, churchmen, politicians, professional or quasi-professional workers, all likely to know the local housing scene. Such contact would have allowed key themes and questions to emerge to allow more organised contact with a 'representative' group of the local population and with those managers identified as 'significant'. Within the local population the researchers would probably anticipate doing a fairly large-scale survey involving one of the commercial firms who organise and manage questionnaire-based surveys.

A particularly devoted researcher might carry out pilot interviews to ensure that the chosen items for questioning are intelligible and relevant. The range of questions might include some factual questions about housing situation and history, some more attitudinal questions about the meaning of the themes and processes under investigation and some profile questions to enable the surveyed population to be grouped into some socio-economic categories, age, nationality or other group-ings to aid discussion of findings and as a basis for explanation. While this work was in progress the researcher might be making contact with those managerial informants whose front doors are not so easily identifiable. With these, depending on the form of access granted/ negotiated, a formal interview might be sought during which the researcher would raise topics and invite discussion to allow a schedule to be completed. Essentially both sets of informants would be asked about their relations with each other and the social researcher's task is to find the right questions and to record the answers as comprehensively as possible.

In our experience it is more and more common for researchers to rely on others to do the mass of actual contact with informants and to receive for analysis and processing merely the results of that organised contact. As fashion has valued more elaborate, quantifiable and 'scientific' research so that processing has become more often than not a computer process; and that end-point frequently and inevitably influences the form and content of the earlier stages of the enquiry. For example, questions have to be asked and answered in a form which the computer can analyse.

At the end of empirical work in this conventional enquiry into the nature of social relations existing between local urban populations and those who manage their access to housing, the researcher would have the results of the neighbourhood surveys and of the interviews with managers which would be 'played back', as it were, into the researcher's own knowledge and understanding of the over-all and specific housing situation to allow 'findings' to emerge.

The advantages of these methods are that research is manageable, data will emerge, analysis can proceed and with reasonable economy quite a large-scale study can be planned. We have hinted at our basic dissatisfaction with the method; typically it means that the researcher is a manager of data-collectors, a programmer and reader of computer data, someone committed to making sense out of a particular form of data which does not require the involvement between the sociologist and his human subject matter. However, our criticism is not restricted to, or even mainly with, the computerised technology which has overtaken so much social research, for it was also the case in our experience that the questionnaire survey had become an over-utilised tool of applied social research, particularly in the obvious 'problem areas' of towns and cities – so much so that in our kind of neigh-bourhoods the response 'Oh, not another survey!' had to be anticipated and hence an alternative sought.

We were also influenced by the criticism of those phenomenologically orientated sociologists for whom the crucial problem in sociological method lies with *meaning*: how can sociology reveal/get at the meaning and significance people attach to those relationships which the sociologist has selected as significant, and more generally how do people make sense of, and bring order to, their social environment and translate that understanding into action? Such concerns are central to what has been termed 'the action frame of reference' (see pp. 5–6 above). The questionnaire approach, as Cicourel (1964) demonstrates, fails to confront critical problems of meanings and interpersonal relations. Too easily the questionnaire can be a means of imposing the terminology, interests and understanding of the researcher on those whose understanding, interests and terminology the sociologist should be concerned to discover. Handbooks of research design impress on surveyors the need for standardisation of responses and questions, of techniques for establishing *rapport*, of the care and delicacy in utilising 'probe' questions. The *rapport* and probes are all essential to maintain the interviewee's acceptance to being asked questions in the first place and his continuing to answer them *in the approved fashion*. This feature of questionnaires is particularly influential in social research which is concerned with quantification and measurement. Frequently the use of questionnaires and measurement scales itself creates a system of 'measured objects', doing little more than reveal to their users only what *was measurable*, about which the researchers wished to learn – what Cicourel (1964) termed 'measurement by fiat'.

Undoubtedly, when used properly and sensibly, questionnaire surveys can be a valid and useful tool for social research. However, it is necessary to relate method to the actual context of social action under study. In our research forms of the questionnaire were used on specific occasions for specific purposes, but not as a means for investigating the understandings and meanings of our 'informants', nor for the task of discovering the social relations between them and the managers.

Another problem of the questionnaire/interview method is that it very much depends on memory of past events and is not of much value to the study of on-going processes; a series of surveys or interviews can take a series of 'snapshots' through a process but is unsuitable if the main purpose of study is to examine the process, not just the outcome. Our pilot-stage research convinced us that too little was known in detail about the process of housing allocation, redevelopment, area-improvement decisions, and the like, to rely on 'stage' surveys or interviews. Further, in order to avoid the fallibility of human memory and the tendency for *ex post facto* rationalisation to distort the data, alternative methods had to be sought.

Participant Observation: an Alternative?

The method, known as 'participant observation', stands in contrast to the formal interview/survey-based method we have been discussing. The participant observer 'joins the group he is studying as a member and attempts to be at one and the same time one of the observed as well as the observer' (Stacey, 1969, p. 50). Such a role implies some commitment to involvement in the activity and processes under study, but the participant observer's contribution to group life is likely to be minimal, sufficient to maintain his legitimacy as group member but not as leader or initiator. He attempts to cause as little change as possible in the milieu in which he studies so that what he finds out and understands is 'real' and not merely the effect of his presence.

This mode of research was not directly applicable to our purposes.

First, our experience had taught us that in the areas and neighbourhoods whose housing processes interested us, there were few groups of any kind, and fewer still with a concern with housing issues, and none at all in which the participation of a male university-trained and - employed sociologist would have been other than a most extraordinary event. So, with whom could we 'participate'? Second, we were not in business to do a 'community study', as our concern was not so much with intra-community relationships – the typical concern of such studies – but with a relationship we suspected to be somewhat remote, indirect and structured by bureaucratic organisation: in short, the relationships between residents and housing 'managers'. We did not have the time for the gradual task of familiarisation and acceptance which a community study requires. Finally, we knew our neighbourhoods to be fragmented and disparate and lacking the boundaries and cohesion expected or implied in the word 'community'.

However, early on in our work we were encouraged that two other sociologists, Jon Gower Davies (1972) and Norman Dennis (1972), had confronted some of the problems of method that we are discussing by becoming involved in an active way in a number of relationships and processes which they wished to interpret and understand. Davies, in Newcastle, gained access to a range of data about the city council's intentions for the 'revitalisation' of an inner-city neighbourhood through his active participation with some local residents about local issues. Dennis, in Sunderland, having despaired of 'finding out' by conventional research methods what really happens, documented the experiences which he shared with his neighbours in their attempts to 'participate' with the planners over urban renewal. As secretary to a residents' association, Dennis's front-line involvement provided a rich source of data in itself and provided opportunities for obtaining other information which contributed to his intriguing account of urban processes and planning.

These studies encouraged us in a form of research enquiry whereby we had become closely involved as activists in neighbourhood associations in the hope that the experiences of such action would provide data for our research which neither of the conventional approaches would allow. We sought to break down the distinctions conventionally drawn between action and research, and to distinguish our approach from 'action research' we use the term 'research – action'.

From Action Research to 'Research–Action'

One definition of 'action research' suggests an aim 'to contribute both to the practical concerns of people in an immediate problematic situation and to the goals of social science by joint collaboration within a mutually acceptable ethical framework' (Rapoport, 1970). Here the activists and the researchers are different people: the researchers are consultants, advisers, monitors of processes, but they are not direct participants in the implementation of action geared to change or remedy the problematic situation.

Research–action on the other hand is based on the assumption that direct involvement and participation will provide cues and clues to the meaning for the paricipants of the process and its outcome. Research action is perhaps not so much a method as an orientation or a perspective which permits the utilisation of survey, interview and questionnaire techniques and, indeed, also modes of participant observation. Such techniques, however, are used not to generate data for analysis elsewhere but to provide materials for use within the social context of the research, to aid and abet discussion, argument and action among the participants.

Research–action presumes a somewhat different relationship between researcher and researched than do conventional methods. In order to achieve doorstep *rapport* or interviewee assent the conventional researcher frequently has to make claims about the aims and purposes of the enquiry. The data so obtained are then carried away and used for purposes frequently remote from those used to ease its gathering. Contact is fleeting and transitory. Our hope was that through our rather different relationship between researcher and researched we would be able to observe what happened and how people acted and reacted with greater directness than occurs in that conventional research which proceeds by asking questions about past events and thus finds difficulty in separating out attitude, hope, distortion, forgetfulness and invention in people's response. Most research proceeds in a somewhat predatory way, seizing data from one social situation and analysing them with the aid of the machinery and procedures of another. We were seeking an understanding both of the structural bases of society in terms of the distribution of economic and political power at a local level and of belief systems and patterns of meaning which operate in day-to-day relationships and affect the way power is translated from potentiality to actuality. This is entailed in any study of social relations between power groups. But the crucial problem for research is to *make visible* and then *understand* how individuals define such relations, how they categorise others and make sense of their social environment and how that understanding is translated into action.

We are aware that any success we have had in coming to terms with this problem is only partial, but we do believe that our method provides a valid and necessary means to approaching it.

Research–Action and Inner-City Housing Problems

Our concern was with housing, specifically with differential access to housing and the activities of those with power to influence housing opportunities. We have had to try and make clear the day-to-day routine process of allocation, the implementation of rules, discretion and the meaning that these processes had for those they affected. In order to avoid mere replication of official accounts of these processes, we sought to view 'real-life' management processes, and find out what actually happens rather than what people say happens. We have not therefore carried out interviews and surveys of representatives of 'each side' about contacts and relationships, for they can never be the same as actual observations and experiences of those contacts. A pilot stage of the research entailed negotiations with a variety of neighbourhood groups and associations in which we sought to provide a useful service to these organisations in return for something of a privileged insider's view of what happened. We did not pose as neutral researchers. We could not, at the outset, specify with whom contact would be achieved or in detail what would be the outcome. We were confident, however, that our involvement would provide a rich source of experience upon which a viable sociology depends.

The neighbourhoods and the associations with whom a research-action involvement was negotiated will be described in detail in the chapters which follow. But to round off this discussion of the methods used in the enquiry as a whole some general comments may be appropriate. In each chapter we have tried to specify how the research-action roles undertaken by the authors influenced both 'what happened' and what we could find out about 'what happened'. We are very aware that the nature of the involvement influenced our data and we need to make clear in what ways that occurred. We would criticise both Davies and Dennis for failing to explore in sufficient detail this aspect in their accounts. For instance, the reader of Dennis's book will find that only in a footnote is the identity of the author as Secretary of the Residents' Association admitted. The Secretary is the chief actor in the tale . . . but how little we know about him! (Paris and Blackaby, 1973).

It will be apparent that the associations with whom we worked were a varied bunch, frequently with ill-defined goals and aims, and having a somewhat precarious existence. All, however, could be described as attempting to serve the interests of the relatively poor or powerless in their area. By various means of advice and organisation they attempted to help such people become more capable and powerful in bargaining with 'urban managers'. They sought to test the system, exploit the use of discretion and to bring about changes in the rules and procedures by which 'managers' allocated their resources. Theirs was a role of mediation, therefore, between 'managed' and 'managers'.

The associations were all financially and organisationally independent of the city council. Some relied on charitable finance; others were purely 'voluntary', only requiring 'servicing' from other neighbourhood agencies. Most combined the 'case-work' approach of housing, planning and welfare rights advice with 'community work' with groups of residents.

Research – action with neighbourhood groups has involved two loose sorts of role: that of housing/planning adviser to enquirers who called at the association's office, centre or base; and that of participant in residents' group activities. To both the enquirers and residents the researchers were seen as *activists* – adviser, community worker, or perhaps a more vague definition, the man from the 'association' or from the 'housing place'. To the co-workers at the association, the researchers were both 'researcher' and 'activist', for it had always been made clear that there was a research interest in the involvement. Usually the researchers were regarded as equal co-workers who were good at finding things out, knowledgeable about housing and planning, and it was accepted that certain sorts of research and action were legitimate kinds of activity.

Throughout their involvement, therefore, the researchers met and spoke to several sorts of people: the residents and enquirers who made themselves known to the associations, the staff of the associations, various 'urban managers' – officers in housing, planning, public health and other departments of the city council – as well as a number of landlords, estate agents and housing association workers.

The nature of our involvement was such that it precluded any attempt to question a representative sample of residents in any neighbourhood. The aims and reputations of each neighbourhood association meant that they have only achieved contact with some of the population in their area. Associations committed to 'saving' and 'improving' houses, for instance, may not, after an initial burst of protest, see much of those who want the area pulled down. Housing-advice centres will never meet those who do not hear of their services or those who know about and can 'play the system' effectively for themselves.

In planning the research we had considered attempting to describe something of the social composition of our areas by using more comprehensive methods than our research–action involvement. For this purpose we examined data derived from the 1971 census, but found its relevance questionable in the light of both on-going changes in the neighbourhoods and the quite different kinds of data which became available to us. Of more relevance was our limited involvement in small surveys in some of our areas and, to a certain extent, the information they have derived is a corrective to what may be a more narrow and limited view gained from research–action. All of these surveys were designed specifically with 'action' in mind, and in most cases they were initiated not by ourselves but by those with whom we worked. We were, and continue to be, sceptical of the validity of many of the responses that were derived on attitudes and intentions but less so about the more 'hard' types of data – tenure, family size and composition – and as such the surveys have been of some use in providing a general picture with which we can compare and supplement our other data.

A critical feature of our involvement has been the distinctive nature of the relatioships we have shared with those from whom we have obtained information. Like all research relationships, what can be found out is influenced by the nature of the expectations held of the researcher by those he is researching. Earlier, we rejected any notion of research that wrested the researcher from a context of social interaction. In our work, what our informants said and did was very much a product of whom they thought we were and what we could do. As we have noted, most, if not all, saw us as housing advisers and community workers. For the adviser this expectation is crucial, for many thought that this role implied an ability to distribute resources, and this had a considerable effect on the relationships that became established. This was especially so in the study that dealt with allocating council and housing association tenancies. Here the researcher/adviser came to appreciate better the invidious position of one who is actually a gatekeeper to resources. He learned what it was like to account for the rules, the shortage, the possibilities of help, and how, effectively, to say 'yes' to some and 'no' to others. But he, like the other researchers, was also able to develop a critical faculty on what was likely or plausible about what people said as well as an accomplished ability to get people to talk about matters that they might once have thought irrelevant.

Each of the research-action roles entailed elements of community work, defined as some conscious effort by the worker to engage and involve residents in the particular locality in activities geared to their collective benefit. Understandably, the researchers brought distinctive ideas to bear within their own role, and a general indication of our working ideology and approach to action should now be specified to help the reader understand our endeavours.

The existing system of resource distribution is inegalitarian but permits, at any rate in principle, many benefits as of *right*. Rights, however, often need to be fought for in order that the principle be translated into practice, and because of the complexity of provision well-informed advocates/advisers are needed to see that people receive the benefits to which they are entitled. At one level of analysis it is the inefficiency and ideologies of the officer structure in the various bureaucracies that restrict resource distribution. People do not get their rights because officers cannot or will not deliver them. But we would propose a stronger analysis which maintains that inefficiency and cussedness are not individual faults or errors but are rather intrinsic characteristics of the same system of resource allocation. This analysis places much greater strength on what the officers in the bureaucracies *could not* do because of outside constraints rather than what they *would not* do. This stronger analysis goes on to suggest that only partial change will occur if better advice is available to individual people. What is required is a process of politicising groups of people and demonstrating publicly that whole sections of the population do not receive the benefits that are promised them by the Welfare State. Politicisation and subsequent action would then seek fundamental change in the basis on which the system of resource distribution depends, not just adjustments in the discretionary or formal rules governing officers.

As the work developed we came to stress the latter kind of analysis, although we found constantly, as we shall reveal in later chapters, that the pressure and ambiguities of day-to-day work predicated against the adoption of the kinds of action and organisation that this analysis would suggest are necessary.

Our research action proceeded for a period of about two years; there was only a formal starting date and finishing date dictated by the exigencies or research funding, not by the work in hand. In many instances our involvement continued well after the 'research' had stopped. So, in this time, we worked in our selected neighbourhoods responding to the day-to-day demands of the work, seeking to memorise and record as much as was possible of our experience and never being quite sure what would prove valuable when we came to make sense of our findings. Our 'raw data' consisted of many notes and jottings, case sheets from the advice centres, minutes, reports, interview typescripts and much that remained in our heads until we came to write up our experiences. We had to bring together and make sense of this extremely varied data. Fortunately we were all sufficiently aware of the background and assumptions of each neighbourhood project to make the processing of our raw material into data a collective effort through discussion, writing, rewriting and more and more discussion. Sociologically we faced the same problem that faces other researchers using similar techniques — which Howard Becker has recently summed up as follows (Becker, 1971a, p. 26):

Observational research produces an immense amount of detailed description. . . . Faced with such a quantity of 'rich' but varied data, the researcher faces the problem of how to analyze it systematically and then to present his conclusions so as to convince other scientists of their validity. Participant observation . . . has not done well with this problem, and the full weight of evidence for conclusions and the processes by which they were reached are usually not presented, so that the reader finds it difficult to make his own assessment of them and must rely on his faith in the researcher.

Whether the accounts which follow are convincing or not will, of course, depend on the assumptions and knowledge readers bring to our material. In this section and in the previous chapter we have tried to make explicit some of the ideas and views which have led us to select some instances, examples and events from many to make what is hopefully a coherent and interesting story. We are very much aware that our method and approach greatly influenced the data upon which this writing is based and we are unlikely to convince those who believe that replicability is the keynote for valid and accurate social research.

BIRMINGHAM: THE CONTEXT FOR THE CASE STUDIES

Birmingham's council-housing achievement is its pride and joy. The city council is the largest municipal landlord in the country, perhaps in Western Europe. In 1974 the council owned and managed over 143,000 dwellings: more than 40 per cent of the city's households paid rent to the council; net rental income was in excess of £20 million. So substantial a housing stock spread throughout the city's area and beyond could hardly fail to exert a major influence over the city's total housing situation.

The extent of the publicly owned sector in Birmingham is the more remarkable when it is realised that apart from a handful of dwellings it has all been built since 1920. Although Birmingham in the late nineteenth century was synonymous with municipal enterprise, notably in the field of gas and water services for the 'common good' of its citizens, housing was not among its pioneering undertakings. The city's famed central clearance scheme of the 1860s did not provide alternative accommodation for those displaced from the slums and hovels to make way for the grandeur that was Corporation Street. They had to make out with whatever the market then provided. However, the city's public works department regulated the extent and shape of private building within the city, and the development of extensive areas of workmen's houses, interspersed with sections of grander housing for the middle and upper classes, in an arc around the city centre was municipally planned but financed and owned by private enterprise. Between 1858 and 1890 some 45,000 houses were built in this way (Briggs, 1952).

Despite enabling legislation and clear evidence of worsening conditions and acute shortages by 1914, the cost of house-building deterred the corporation from action. Only when the post-war legislation of 1919 and 1923 provided improved subsidies for council building did the city's programme get under way, making rapid progress after 1925. In 1930 some 6687 council houses were built (that figure was not reached again until 1967); by 1933 40,000 council houses had been built, 50,000 by 1939. As in other cities, the major emphasis on housing provision in the 1930s was that built for owner-occupation: some 50,000 houses were privately built in Birmingham between 1930 and 1939. The characteristic lay-out for private and council houses was one of spacious estates, each house having a sizeable garden, with shops and other facilities set on main traffic routes (MacMorran, 1973).

By 1939 the city council had started on an extensive slum-clearance project and when war broke out was poised to undertake the comprehensive redevelopment of central-area housing. If actual building was delayed by the war, the city influenced and took full advantage of wartime legislation which facilitated the compulsory acquisition of large areas of old slum property, and peripheral land was available within the city's boundaries for the new building needed to rehouse those from the central slums and so allow a progressive comprehensive redevelopment and housing programme to be undertaken.

However, in the immediate post-war period shortage of materials and labour and pressing and urgent demands for housing of any sort meant that there could be no start on such grandiose schemes. Birmingham's post-war housing drive was slow to start. By 1949 only about 4000 houses had been built; a major emphasis in local housing policy was the basic repair of old houses scheduled for redevelopment so that they could be fully utilised until slum clearance could commence. In the post-war period the register of those queueing for a home in the city increased rapidly, reaching 65,000 in 1948. Even by instituting a five-year work or residence qualification (which remains to the present) the register still numbered 43,000 in 1952. Repair and renovation of old houses, with new building representing additional rather than replacement housing, continued until 1955. However, from 1950 to 1955 there was a greatly improved rate of house-building (over 18,000) and a new problem was emerging: land shortage.

Most of the developments in the decade after 1945 were at densities similar to those of the interwar period, such that available reserves of land were rapidly reduced. In 1955 the national subsidy system was altered to favour slum clearance rather than general needs as a target of council housing programmes. In Birmingham in the period 1956–60 some 11,700 new houses were constructed by the council and as a result land for further new building in the central-area comprehensive development areas (C.D.A.s) was made possible (Sutcliffe and Smith, 1974).

The form of development in these areas in the early 1960s was influenced by other changes in subsidies, fashion among architects, and the building industry, which favoured high-rise developments. From 1964 the council also benefited from the easing of restrictions on building outside its boundaries and from the acquisition of some large sites for development within the city boundaries. In the decade 1960 – 70, no fewer than 52,407 council housing units were built. It was this great surge in council building which made possible the completion of the five great central-area redevelopment schemes and the implementation of a second phase of inner-city redevelopment in areas adjoining the C.D.A.s with a target date of 1975 for completion. Peripheral developments at Chelmsley Wood (and others scheduled in North Worcestershire), other developments at Castle Vale and Bromford Bridge and proposals for the Woodgate Valley within the city gave rise to an air of optimism in 1970 that the housing problem was controlled, if not beaten. The waiting list had been reduced from a 1955 high of 64,000 to 20,000 during a period when 50,000 families had been rehoused from the slums. As the housing committee's Annual Report for 1970 stated:

> The Council will be well aware of the magnitude of the housing problems facing the City. The excellent house building achievements of the last few years have enabled the Housing Committee to make considerable progress in their task of dealing with the huge accumulation of slum properties in the City, nearly 17,000 of which have been demolished during the last three years. The Committee are confident that at the present rate of progress (and assuming that sufficient land for new housing is forthcoming) they will be able to deal with the remainder by the end of 1975.

Such was the situation when we embarked on our explorations. The neighbourhoods in which we became involved in different ways were greatly influenced by council policy. Any complacency or even optimism that council officials or members may have had in 1970 would have wilted rapidly in the situations we found.

In the north of the city, as we became involved in the provision of housing advice and aid, it was apparent that for many families the wait for decent housing had been a long one already and, on investigation, it became clear that their wait would go on. In the south, our work revealed the agonisingly slow process of redevelopment. This process had left large tracts of partially cleared land derelict, dangerous and undeveloped. We also saw the faltering and uncertain first effects of the 1969 Housing Act, which promised a better future for our older houses by means of improvement.

Were these situations merely little local difficulties or rather particularly local expressions of a more general situation? It would be true to say that there was not and had not been much extensive criticism of what was occurring locally; the city council could and did refer critics to its record.

By 1975 the situation had changed drastically: the slum-clearance programme had faltered; in places it was being subject to drastic revision; council-house building had gone through one of its worst phases, and the housing register had risen steadily and was in excess of 30,000.

The four case studies which follow report how various kinds of neighbourhood associations were able to influence the housing opportunities available to residents in those neighbourhoods. In one of those neighbourhoods we were able to explore something of the process whereby those on the housing register waited and were (or were not) allocated a council house. In another we observed something of the process of slum clearance in one of those areas confidently designated in 1955 for eventual redevelopment and which remains at the time of writing a chaos and eyesore of old houses, new houses, cleared sites and derelict land. In a third area, an alternative to municipal slum clearance and the encouragement of owners to improve their own houses was being essayed – but, as we record, the influence of the city's housing policy was of crucial importance. In another case study we look in detail at some houses on the edge of a comprehensive redevelopment area which were saved from clearance.

The typical neighbourhood, of course, does not exist and a great many of Birmingham's neighbourhoods are very different from those described here. But what we observed in these areas of older housing was clearly part of a more general process. We became aware of similar features in other redevelopment and improvement areas in the city and were struck by the way accounts from other towns and cities – provided by the community development projects, inner-area studies, by Shelter and in the pages of *Community Action* – described similar tendencies in the processes of urban renewal and housing allocation. In this respect what can be discerned in our case studies is the working out of central and local government housing policy and practice and so from each can be gleaned a better understanding of the city's and the country's housing question.

Chapter 3

Case Study 1: Queueing for a Home

Council House Allocation in Birmingham

Above we have sketched the development and the size of Birmingham's housing stock, whose creation and ádministration has been so predominant a feature of the city's government. The housing stock ranges widely in age, size and type and is situated within the city's fifty miles of boundary and beyond.

Partly because of the heterogeneous nature of the municipal stock, but also as a result of persistent over-all shortages, complex administrative structures and allocation procedures have been devised to determine who gets which council tenancy, where, and when. These were changing as our study progressed and we have drawn attention to some of them. After our research ended and resulting from a thorough review by the council's performance review committee, other changes were made. So our account is no longer valid in detailed aspects. But the changes made in no way reduce the complexity, the general nature of the process, the scale of the undertaking, or the necessity for many applicants to wait in a queue for a decent home.

In 1974 the city council owned and managed over 143,000 dwellings comprised largely of council-built houses and flats on estates (131,909) but also including 'various properties' bought out of private ownership (7853), dwellings in slum clearance and redevelopment areas pending demolition (2129) and temporary bungalows or 'prefabs' (1797). In the same year over 7000 of these dwellings became available for letting; this availability resulted from new building, acquisition and from relets, the latter occurring due to vacancies in the existing stock as tenants die, leave, or are evicted.

The allocation of the municipal stock is managed according to departmental definitions of different categories of demand. Based upon the types of vacancies that occur and an order of priorities assessed (between the need to rehouse families displaced by slum clearance, homeless families, families who have registered housing need and other categories of demand), every year the Housing Committee decides in advance roughly how many properties will go to which type of demand. At the same time a vigorous effort is made to match, through an elaborate transfer system, household size and structure to an appropriate type of accommodation.

While many people have been rehoused during the process of redevelopment, a substantial number of families, not affected by slum clearance, are taken into the municipal sector every year after serving their term on what is popularly called the 'waiting list', but officially designated as the 'housing register'. On the whole, however, families in areas subject to slum clearance action receive priority as a category of demand in any one year over applicants on the waiting list. This is because sites have to be cleared to schedule, and in order to ensure that families are moved out in time the housing department frequently has to offer accommodation that approximates nearest to the wishes of the people involved. Thus this section of demand often commands priority access to the more popular estates and types of property that are available.

The 'waiting list' or housing register is itself a fairly elaborate apparatus. By no means every person or family in housing need or waiting for an adequate home is on the list. In Birmingham, while a family can register need on arrival to the city to live or work, for their first five years they are simply recorded on a 'register of enquiries'. Only those who maintain contact will achieve the 'general section' of the register, although a family who did not register initially may be able to prove eligibility for this. Only those on the general section will normally stand a chance of an offer of a council house and then not until they have been on the list for at least six months. The most important criterion in making allocations is the length of time a person has been registered, for points for waiting time are awarded from the time of registration. Applicants on the general section may gain additional points based on various types of housing need – amenities at present home, overcrowding, extent of sharing. Special medical needs and forms of war service will earn an applicant family additional points. In addition, all applicant families are graded on the basis of subjective assessments by housing visitors of their housekeeping standards and rent-paying ability for broad types of property: 'older type', 'interwar' and 'modern' were the terms used at the time of our study; in 1974 the terms were amended to 'good', 'medium' and 'poor', and subsequently the formal grading scheme has been abolished.

Since different housing estates and city areas enjoy different levels of popularity according to their age, style, rent level, accessibility, reputation, etc., each has in effect a different points 'threshold' for offers which influences the availability to applicants.

Council house lettings therefore involve a complex balancing between various elements of supply and demand. None of these is constant over time. Between 1970 and 1974 there was a fall in the number of new buildings coming available each year; there was a smaller fall in the numbers who had to be rehoused due to slum clearance; so applicants on the general section had fewer opportunities for offers. An increase in emergency homelessness in the period meant, in practical terms, a further reduction in the number of lettings for these applicants. The number of casual vacancies from the housing stock was fairly constant in the period, but there was a sharp increase in the number of applicants. So in the period of our study there was more pressure on the waiting list and fewer (both numerically and relative to other categories of housing need) lettings to waiting list applicants.

To manage this housing stock and this complex allocation system requires a substantial administrative unit. At the time of this study there were the first moves in Birmingham towards a decentralised housing-management system, but for all practical purposes the administration was based within Bush House, a city-centre office block. Within Bush House, management was divided among a number of sections, reflecting both the various functions – *rent collection, repairs, transfers and exchanges*, etc. – and the various 'demand groups' for allocation – *ordinary applications, rehousing/slum clearance, homelessness*. Broadly speaking these sections would 'bid' for keys becoming available for letting, a process supervised by a senior administrative officer. A *lettings section* communicated the results of successful bids to the lucky applicants, who would be called to attend at Bush House. A section for *housing visitors* administered the various kinds of direct contact needed between these various sections and tenants and applicants. There was also a *liaison section* which could take up special cases referred by councillors, or to a lesser extent by other organisations like advice centres. It was policy that casual callers at Bush House should be interviewed if they so wished and the day-to-day routine is such that Bush House is a crowded place of many applicants of various sorts waiting in none-too-comfortable surroundings to discuss their situation with a clerk from one of the sections. It should be appreciated that given the volume of work – the huge number of those eligible to register, the number being affected by slum clearance and the daily pressures and risks of homelessness – the number of files stored in Bush House is immense and the problems of providing a personalised administration quite intense. The capacity of clerks to locate files to answer particular queries for casual callers was limited to say the least, although those attending by appointment could expect better. It is no exaggeration to say that in the period of our study the reputation of the housing department for careful and sensitive control of the 'personal' side of housing management was poor in the extreme. Major changes under way in the period indicated an awareness by senior management and the housing committee that this was indeed the case.

Here then was the context for our first case study.

The Area

Those queueing for a council house are to be found among the city's furnished and unfurnished lettings. As slum clearance has proceeded and as the trend to suburbanised owner-occupation has continued, such lettings only occur in certain fairly well-defined areas of the city in the middle ring among the semi-detached and terraced houses built in late Victorian and Edwardian times – housing which, when first built, was among the most elegant in the city. The area of our first case study is a large tract to the north and west of Birmingham's city centre, beyond part of the council's redeveloped 'Corporation Town' and before a large park and modern spacious housing. The houses have two, or sometimes three, storeys and are built in terraces, but typically they are more spacious than in other neighbourhoods. Only in a few patches are there crowded, old houses and back terraces. Most properties have front and back gardens; streets curve almost graciously and are often tree-lined.

When first built these houses provided homes for the manufacturers and businessmen of Birmingham and the Black Country, and for workmen, mostly skilled artisans, from neighbouring factories. Most of the area did not join Birmingham until 1911 and, until then, it must have retained a certain village independence. In the interwar period, its incorporation into the city was completed as new houses were built on available sites – a mixture of neat semi-detached and grander detached houses, mostly private, with some scattered patches of more modern council houses. Since 1950 there has been little building in the area except in the southern part, bordering a comprehensive development area. There has been limited planning activity and, apart from some small areas affected by road improvement, no 'blight' on the area. A fairly busy market for houses has been maintained and many of the houses have all the basic amenities, often in recent years aided by the availability of grants. Since the announcement of the council's new urban renewal policy in 1973 most of the area has been given the stability of designated or proposed General Improvement Area status, although some parts to the south have become the more problematic 'renewal areas' and are to be declared Housing Action Areas under the 1974 Housing Act.

It would be incorrect, however, to suggest that this is a homogenous and settled residential district. Most of the former middle-class and professional owners have left, and their houses often subdivided, such that this is part of the city's pool of relatively cheap privately rented housing. Most of the small artisans' dwellings remain and continue to provide fairly inexpensive houses for the owner-occupation of both an immigrant and indigenous working class.

During the pilot phase of the research a survey, broadly covering the area of interest, found 66 per cent of heads of households in manual socio-economic groups and a further 20 per cent were not employed or had retired: 57 per cent of householders were owner-occupiers; 22 per cent unfurnished tenants; and 13 per cent furnished tenants (in August 1974 the new Rent Act came into force and partly replaced the difference between furnished and unfurnished tenancies by a new, critical distinction between tenancies with residential and non-residential landlords – as much of our empirical work took place before this time, we shall continue to refer simply to 'furnished' and unfurnished' tenancies); 17 per cent of households were in shared accommodation.

The area is known for being an immigrant area. The same survey found 22 per cent of households Caribbean in origin; 13 per cent from Asian countries; 9 per cent from Eire and Northern Ireland; and 15 per cent from other parts of the British Isles. Cause and effect are of course very difficult to disentangle, but the relative low cost of houses to buy, their availability, their proximity to areas of employment and rented accommodation and the suitability of many houses for part-renting to lodgers are among the factors which have kept the area popular among those groups for whom other housing options are closed.

The cost of housing, its diversity and the mixture of house sizes has meant that it has been one of the relatively few areas in the city where furnished lettings have maintained a significant level, although never enough to meet demand. It is an area in which housing associations have been active in improving and converting older larger houses for working-class tenants.

The Setting for Research–Action

It was in relation to the work of a housing association that our research–action was undertaken. At the outset of our study the association had about ninety tenants and a waiting list of 250. It anticipated quite rapid growth but was aware that it had little knowledge about applicants and about other housing opportunities that existed. It was an association which hoped to be a local area resource centre and to be responsive to, and respected by, its locality. The idea of a housing advice centre linked to a local community organisation emerged from discussions between the researchers, the association staff and the community organisation. It was launched in 1972 and if the number of callers is anything to go by it indeed fulfilled a need.

Housing and advice centres, both run voluntarily and by local authorities, have now become an established feature of many inner urban areas; but the proliferation has been accompanied by diversity, for the activities actually carried out by housing advisers varies not only between such centres but between different advisers within the same centre. Broadly, however, we can distinguish between the straightforward giving of 'information', 'advice' and 'aid'. At the advice centre in our area there were few people who came who just wanted information;

almost invariably they expected more. For example, there were many who wanted to know what they should do to force their landlord to do repairs or who were not sure of what to do on receiving a notice to quit. Most enquirers expected more than an explanation and expected the advice centre workers to take up their case and contact the landlord, public health department, or rent tribunal, etc. Similarly, those with queries about a council-house application wanted the adviser to 'get on to' the housing department and find out what was happening.

Initially the advice centre was concerned with rationalising the tenant selection of the housing association; an early assumption was to ensure that the association gave priority to those in most need – in this way the advisers had a direct role in housing provision and housing aid. The corollary of this was that there were many callers who were unlikely to be rehoused by the association for a long time, if at all. To help these people it was essential to explore fully all the other opportunities that might exist to improve their housing conditions, either where they were, or by moving to different accommodation.

The advice centre workers used a standard 'case sheet' to collect the information necessary for establishing a caller's situation. The aim throughout the interview, though, was to provide a friendly and informal atmosphere, combining questions with the general flow of conversation. In order to give advice it was essential that the workers acquired a good understanding of the workings of the housing department and its rules of housing allocation and eligibility. The process of investigating the circumstances of particular applicants' cases entailed a great many telephone conversations and letters on behalf of individuals and recording the results of these discussions on their 'case sheets'.

Here then, was the setting for the case study: the housing association, the advice centre and the stream of callers in housing need in the locality which provided the means of bringing into focus a wide range of housing issues and the way individuals and organisations sought to tackle them.

Interviewing enquirers, contact with various housing managers, the sharing of information and experience with other advisers were the routine elements of the adviser's work. But the process of giving advice was also a learning process. The adviser found out not just about his 'clients' but also about the nature of the local housing market, as well as the complexity of the council's housing-allocation system. What follows is derived from this particular experience.

Queueing for a Home: the Local Milieu

Whatever optimism and confidence existed in 1972 that the city's over-all housing shortage was beaten dissipated between 1972 and 1975 as the council's house-building programme slumped, house prices soared, and the council's waiting list grew and grew. For the callers at the advice centre, however, there had always been shortage. Most told the advice centre workers of how they had been searching for decent accommodation for many years. Many were on the council's waiting list and the severe shortage of property for letting meant long years of living in small, insecure, ill-repaired and overcrowded rooms with shared facilities. During the twenty-seven months of our involvement, nearly 1100 callers visited the advice centre. Many of these returned several times for further advice or to present further difficulties. Nearly 70 per cent of the callers were private tenants, mostly furnished, and nearly a fifth were lodging with friends or relatives. The remainder were in various kinds of housing need as council tenants in overcrowded or old, ill-repaired properties or owner-occupiers wishing to sell; only five of the callers (less than 1 per cent) were quite literally homeless – the vast majority had a roof over their heads but were seeking somewhere better; 62 per cent of callers were West Indian, either by birth or by parentage, 24 per cent were British, and 5 per cent were Irish. Asians only accounted for 1 per cent of the case load. Most callers represented families (68 per cent), of which just over half were single-parent households. Nearly one-half of all families' eldest children were under 5 years of age.

Over 60 per cent of households had the exclusive use of only one room; nearly 60 per cent lived at densities of over two people per living/bedroom and most households shared or lacked at least one basic facility like a bath or kitchen.

Most privately rented accommodation in our area was not let formally by estate agents or through the columns of the local newspaper. Owners with rooms or flats to let had no trouble in finding tenants. Anyone who lived near a vacant-looking window would be beseiged by callers. Many who were looking for accommodation stopped strangers in the street, knocked on doors at random or kept their eye on the occasional note in a newsagent's window. The role of friends and acquaintances was crucial here as some landlords relied on a system of informal nomination. The availability of rooms also spread by word of mouth and people were lucky if they had a friend in a multi-occupied house who could keep their eye open for one of their neighbours moving out. Sometimes people could find vacant rooms, although the landlord may be asking too much rent; more often he was refusing to take tenants with children. Luck and being around in the right place, at the right time, was crucial.

The housing histories of most enquirers were long, but fairly predictable. Both Birmingham-born families and immigrants would list a series of their previous homes, mostly in the same area and usually of the same sort – one, perhaps two, rented rooms with shared facilities. Nearly 45 per cent of all callers had lived at their present accommodation for less than a year. Some had moved in order to make some marginal improvement in their situation. Others were kept on the move by their landlords wanting to sell the house with vacant possession or requiring the room for his own or a relative's use. Frequently no written notices were issued – mostly landlords gave two or three weeks' verbal warning and many tenants reckoned that the landlord's claim was justified and left. Others did not wish to be so obliging, or may have wanted to move but found other rooms difficult to get, and asked for statutory notices or claimed their rights to temporary security of tenure from the rent tribunal.

Sometimes disputes became bitter, and tenants with resident landlords suffered the most as common entrances, halls and kitchens often provided the scenario for rows, tensions and in some cases violence. Sometimes, the council's 'harassment officer' became involved in these disputes. On occasions he was able to ensure that landlords obeyed the rules; more often, however, even after the enforcement service was improved early in 1974, his visit caused a temporary lapse in the landlord's pressure which was resumed soon after he had left. Even more frequently he was unable to contact a landlord personally and left a standard warning letter that was often ignored. Sometimes rather than give a written notice landlords would merely extend their verbal deadline and give their tenants more time. They would do anything to avoid putting things in writing and making it 'official' – that was inviting 'trouble'.

If most tenants were not long-standing residents at one address, then most had lived in the city for some time. Over 70 per cent had been resident for over five years, and nearly half for over ten years at the time of their first visit to the advice centre.

Most callers were workers, invariably manual labourers, and 64 per cent were actually in work. A few were unemployed or off sick, while about a fifth were not normally at work and were mainly unsupported mothers claiming supplementary benefit. A small number were pensioners or students. Nearly 70 per cent of callers during 1973 had net total household earnings of less than £40 a week. Almost all had either no savings at all, or amounts of less than £100.

Very few people had ever thought seriously about buying a house. A few may have qualified, in terms of income, for a city council mortgage on an older, cheaper house but had insufficient savings to pay the then required minimum deposit of 10 per cent. Others were too old to obtain a mortgage of sufficient length to make monthly repayments bearable. Many householders were simply not earning enough and at the time of our study wives' incomes were not included in the council's calculation unless they were over 40 years of age.

Midway through the research involvement, the city council introduced a new mortgage scheme for newer (post-1935 and, later, post-1925) property. Although many would have welcomed the possibility of 100 per cent mortgages and the inclusion of wives' incomes, irrespective of age, most callers were still not earning enough to pay the price of newer properties, or, if they were, considered that monthly repayments and their existing commitments were far too high for them to face the financial pressure. The adviser and his co-workers frequently encountered resistance to the notion of house purchase from those whose income and savings made them eligible for a mortgage. Some said they would like to own a house, but not for several years. Others simply did not want to buy at all. Very few could consider the prospect at the time of their first visit, and in spite of the adviser's encouragement many of those who could have considered it did not start saving or take any action to make owning a home a possibility.

Here, then, was a setting of poor quality housing, of lack of amenities, of overcrowding and poor relationships with landlords. The prospect of a decent home with security for enquirers at the advice centre rested primarily in eligibility for a council home.

Queueing for a Home: Getting Registered

It sounds very simple. You make your application to the council, and providing you fulfil the necessary employment and residence qualifications you receive your certificate of registration and a preliminary points assessment. Thereafter a housing visitor calls to establish the factual basis for the application, to discuss housing needs, areas of choice and special requirements. Then there is a wait, the length of which depends on a variety of factors and circumstances, before an offer is made and the applicant becomes a council tenant.

At each stage, however, there are a variety of influences at work to make the actual practice of this process far from simple.

Consider registration: although nearly 50 per cent of all callers for advice were registered, a substantial minority (25 per cent) were found to be eligible to go on to the active 'general section' of the register and a further 10 per cent could have registered on the 'record of enquiries', an important but not essential part of registration and a valuable means of building up a good points score. Apart from emphasising the conservative nature of the measure provided by the council waiting list of those in housing need in the city, the experiences and explanations of non-registration were instructive in our developing an understanding of the housing process.

Some of these non-registrants said they had not really thought about getting a council flat. Others were wary of putting their names down for fear of being sent to a distant estate or to a flat in a high tower or, as one Jamaican man put it: 'They never send you to anywhere decent – it is always an old place without a bathroom.' Others claimed that up until they began to experience the problem that had brought them to the advice centre, they had no need of a council flat, although closer questioning would often reveal a long history of sharing facilities, pressure from landlords and overcrowding.

Often, however, no one had ever advised people to register. Usually those who were on the list at the time of their first call to the centre had registered a long time after they had become eligible. Some registered during a time of particular need or crisis, perhaps because their landlord had told them to leave or because their children were arriving from the West Indies. Many regarded the council rather as they would a private landlord. They had visited the housing department to find out whether it could find them somewhere to live immediately, but the situation became redefined as application forms were handed over and they were told that they would have to wait their turn – perhaps it could be two or three years! Some concluded that it was not worth bothering and never completed the form.

Invariably, people had to sort themselves out of the crisis that had led them to register and many almost forgot that they had even put their names down. Some of the enquirers had changed address since and had not kept the department informed of this and of other changes of circumstances. Some were convinced that as the department had not offered accommodation during their time of need, 'they' were not bothered and there seemed little point in persisting.

Once registered and armed with a 'certificate of registration' and a points score, it was still far from clear to applicants what would happen and when. Rarely had they any idea of the relevance of the number of points that they were awarded and how it affected their chances of being rehoused. The role of the housing visitor was also unclear. When one did arrive eventually, many people became optimistic, hoping that the department would now appreciate their need, having actually sent one of its officers to see their housing conditions. Many believed that a lot depended on the visitor and that what he or she said counted; thus it was somehow necessary to convince him or her personally of their need for help.

No small wonder, then, that they sometimes became confused and a little anxious when they saw the visitor inspect bed-clothes and furniture. Few knew why this inspection was carried out. Visitors would discuss an applicant's preferences and would sometimes warn them against naming only those areas where there were few council houses, or estates which were in high demand. Little idea was given about how long an offer would be, how many points were required for offers in different estates and about the exact consequence of naming particular districts in terms of the likely length of wait. Sometimes a comment was made about standards of housekeeping, but not always. Usually the visitor appeared to be in a hurry and left after a few minutes, generally with some assurance, which often confirmed people's feeling of optimism, that she 'will see what she can do'. Even though no promises were made many applicants were convinced that they would soon receive an offer once the visitor had been and had seen how bad their living conditions were. There was invariably a long silence, however, and many began again to fear that the department did not care and that they did not stand much chance of help.

If during the long wait applicants were to enquire, they would be informed of their points score, the queue in which they were placed, the need to notify changes in circumstances, and given the assurance that their turn would come. The fairness of the system in terms of queueing for a turn was emphasised publicly by the chairman of the housing committee in response to some press stories of families who had contrived their own homelessness and 'jumped the queue'. 'Extreme actions,'he said, 'will certainly not entitle people to higher priority.

They will have to wait their turn like everyone else. We have got a fair system of allocation, but it is not an inflexible one, and each case is considered on its individual merits.'

Queueing for a Home: Queueing for What?

As we sought to find out more for and with those seeking a decent home, the complexity of the 'queue' and the idea of waiting their turn became apparent. For it was an odd queue in that the numbers ahead of you was indeterminate and you could not be sure for what it was you were queueing.

An important part of the realisation of the queue's true character rested with the fact that applicants on the general register are only queueing for a proportion of all properties available for letting. Moreover, the proportion appeared to exclude many offers of properties in the most popular areas. These, it seemed, were 'reserved' for another group of prospective tenants, those waiting in clearance areas being redeveloped, and most applicants on the general register were queueing for the least popular of what was available.

This tended to mean that the housing department's stress on area of choice being important was rather different from what it appeared. It was indeed the case that area of choice was a crucial determinant of the speed and likelihood of an offer. Many enquirers lived locally and wanted to continue to live in, or near, the area. Most callers did not have a car and very many laboured in workshops in the neighbourhood, or in one of the metal and engineering factories on the south-eastern edge of the area and towards the city centre, or, and most important, in a large belt of factories and foundries hugging one of the routes to the Black Country. Very many, particularly West Indian families, told the adviser that they did not wish to leave the area because their children were settled and happy in local schools. Most had friends and relatives in the area and were familiar with local shops and their merchandise.

Very few were willing, or indeed able, to change their jobs and this provided the major constraint on 'area of choice'. Most relied on buses which tend to follow the city's radial roads with only intermittent circular or cross-city routes. This rather predetermined modes of access to council estates to and from the place of work. Many would have liked a council house or flat in the area where they were, or at least on one of the few nearby and accessible estates on the post-war redeveloped inner core of the city. These, however, were popular because of their location and in high demand both by families from nearby slum-clearance areas and by other applicants on the list. So most of those who sought advice had the prospect of a long wait.

Often, and to the great confusion of many applicants, offers were made in places outside their stated 'area of choice'. Policy appeared to be that, where possible, applicants should have at least one offer to consider even though it may not be what they wanted. Many rejected these offers without viewing them. Others decided that at least they would *consider* them, and a few even accepted. Often, though, the property offered was so far from their work, perhaps eight miles away on a peripheral estate on the east of the city, three bus rides from places of work on the west. Some were grateful that at least they had an offer, even though it was unacceptable; but for others these unsuitable offers were a further confirmation that the housing department was ignoring their wishes and needs. Few knew why they were not receiving offers of homes where they wanted them. None, apart from the adviser and his colleagues, had told them about the massive 'competition' for offers from the current clearance areas; and only partial attempts had been made to convey the fact that certain areas were more popular and in higher demand than others.

The relationship between the queue and the other demands and various queues for different areas was, therefore, very unclear to most applicants. It was generally known, though, that a preference for a house rather than a flat would ensure a longer wait. Any applicant who stated such a preference would be warned by the visitor that a very long wait would be inevitable. Single people or childless couples who would not consider flats in multi-storeyed blocks were told how difficult it would be to find them other sorts of accommodation. The adviser would confirm these difficulties, although he often found people resistant to changing their minds. Some wanted gardens for their children to play in; others had heard stories about people in high flats being promised a transfer but who had been 'trapped' for years; others were just frightened of heights or of the lifts breaking down. It was the adviser's guess that almost all of their enquirers could only hope for a flat or maisonette, unless they were prepared to wait for many years. Almost every first offer was a flat or maisonette and sometimes the second, third and even fourth. However, only a small minority actually stuck out for a house for very long. Most were prepared to accept a flat or maisonette but, and this was the most important consideration, as long as it was in the right area.

Routine advice given by officers in the housing department was that applicants should 'widen their area of choice' to include those areas where less people were waiting for offers. Sometimes no information was given to the individual applicant about which areas these were; certainly nothing was said about by how much their wait would be reduced, and anyway the areas involved were frequently too far from where people wanted to live and their place of work. The reference to 'widening choice' was essentially misleading since it really meant that the applicants involved had very little choice at all.

Queueing for a Home: Other Complexities

Grading Policy

Areas of choice and preferred types of property became further complicated when the adviser considered the *grading policy* by 'house-keeping standard' and the housing department's division of the housing stock into types roughly according to age.

The advice centre workers became aware of this policy when they received letters marked 'private and confidential' from the housing department telling them that a certain applicant had been considered suitable for property built between the wars and that this type of property only rarely became available. By detailed questioning of clerks in the department and through discussions with colleagues in other advice centres, the workers discovered that there were three, possibly four, different queues for different types of graded accommodation – the form used by the visitors showed that these were 'central area' (C.A.), 'relet' and 'post-war' property. Letters from the department about particular applicants talked of 'old', 'interwar', 'early post-war' and 'post-war' property. Some clerks denied over the telephone that there was a separate category for 'early post-war'; others said that there was.

Very few of the enquirers were graded for 'old property', and those that were seemed doomed to wait for many years for old, substandard clearance-area housing in much need by the department for rehousing 'low-standard' families from areas subject to immediate clearance. Rather more were considered suitable for property built between the wars, which meant very long waits for rare vacancies on an interwar estate, some five miles and two bus rides away from where most enquirers lived, or a very slim chance of a vacancy in a modernised old house or a flat in a converted older house – one of the department's 'various properties'. Again, these sort of properties were in high demand by those in current clearance areas who were requesting houses rather than flats, or property with relatively low rents compared with that built after the war. A few applicants were considered suitable for 'early post-war property', which seemed to mean distant estates to the east or south-west or a part of the earlier post-war redevelopment area to the east of the city centre. The majority of enquirers seemed, however, to be considered suitable for post-war property – which seemed to include some early post-war property – and, occasionally, some with high points received offers of the sort normally used for 'interwar suitability' – mainly miscellaneous older housing converted into flats.

The adviser found some difficulty in conveying this complexity to the enquirers. Sometimes it meant telling people that their standards of housekeeping were 'too good' for the type of property they really wanted! Others had to be told that their standards were deemed not good enough for the sort of property they hoped to get. Most enquirers were angry on learning this. One man's comments were fairly typical: 'they came down to us and went back and told them we didn't keep the place clean, but we try our best. I mean, I'll go and buy a Rembrandt and put it to the wall! There's not much you can do with only one room.' Some directed most of their hostility towards the visitor for not making it clear what she was doing or for not informing them before she arrived so that they could make preparations. Many told the adviser that no improvements were possible given the state of the property and that most furniture and fittings belonged to their landlord and were not their responsibility. Some, however, did try to 'improve' – some decorated, others bought new furniture or changed the sheets on the bed more often. Usually, this was simply to prove to the visitor that they could look after their place well and was not a conscious attempt to improve their chances of an offer.

It was housing department policy that a 'revisit' should occur every six months for anyone graded for property other than 'post-war' but the workers at the advice centre found this rarely adhered to. Usually, however, if they specifically requested a revisit, then one was made, but there was often some delay. Fortunately, most enquirers were regraded for 'post-war' property as a result of the visit – but whether they were or not it all served to confirm the impression that 'they' did not care and were finding excuses for why people would not be given a decent place to live.

Homelessness

A further aspect of the complexity of housing provision was the
realisation that queues, however many there were, could be jumped.
Offers were not only made to those with high points levels but to those,
with children, who became homeless as proved by possession
orders – what we could call 'demonstrable homelessness', or by a
verification carried out by an investigating officer in the applicant's
home – 'negotiated homelessness'. These were the two varieties of
'actionable homelessness' that led to positive intervention by the
council. During the course of their work the adviser and his colleagues
discovered that the annual quota for homeless lettings could be, and
frequently was, exceeded during any one year, with many people thus
'queue-jumping' in a legitimate fashion.

But 'actionable homelessness' was usually achieved only after many
difficulties. Many landlords were unwilling to issue legal notices to quit,
and, if wanting tenants out in order to sell or to move in relatives, their
tenants frequently thought such reasons justified and agreed that the
house *was* the landlord's and that they should leave. Some felt they
'owed the landlord a favour' as he had been kind enough to let them a
room at all; such tenants would often claim to be on good terms with
their landlord. Some landlords did follow the rules, though much time,
patience and negotiation was inevitably required.

Although *tenants* could become 'demonstrably homeless', this was not
the case for the many lodgers or *licencees* who came to the advice centre.
At first, just stopping with friends and relatives on a 'temporary' basis in
the absence of alternatives, they found that 'temporary' could become
quite long term. There was no rent, no proper tenancy and little
prospect of either side agreeing to the county court possession order and
eviction procedure. Going to court was unreasonable 'trouble-making'.

For those who did achieve 'demonstrable homelessness', it usually
meant a long, tense wait until the bailiffs were about to arrive, and then
each case was not treated identically by the housing department. There
was some assessment made of their 'claim on the waiting list'. The
adviser found that, generally, those with less than a year's wait on the
'general section' of the housing register and those who had been evicted
for 'avoidable' reasons, for example they owed the landlord rent (also
those who owed the council rent from an earlier tenancy), tended to be
offered a place in a temporary hostel and then, after a period, they were

usually offered a permanent tenancy, sometimes an old house which was usually the sort reserved for those of the lowest 'suitability grading'. Those 'unavoidably homeless' and with longer claims on the list tended to be offered immediately the sort of accommodation they would have been offered had they remained on the list and waited their turn – for them it was a successful 'queue jump'. A lot seemed to depend, however, on what property was available for letting in the department on the day that their homelessness became 'actionable'.

'Queue-jumping' was seen as 'unfair' in the case of those who engineered homelessness deliberately. Officers would complain that homelessness increased each time publicity was given to it. Popular stories described how people got accommodation by telling the council false stories about their circumstances, and of landlords who deliberately colluded with their tenants. The leader of the city council once gave a public warning to families who were 'engineering evictions': 'there is just a physical limit on the number of homes. . . . We stick closely to the housing list. My advice to anyone trying this method of jumping is – don't' (*Birmingham Evening Mail*, 15 Dec 1973) But the adviser, on the other hand, found that successful 'actionable homelessness' was relatively rare – especially where relatives or friends were anxious to get rid of their lodgers, or mothers their married daughters, few were successful in convincing visiting officers of their intentions. Mostly, situations were redefined – applicants were advised to find their own alternative accommodation in the meantime and to wait their turn for an eventual offer from the council. Sometimes, during these crucial negotiations with officers, applicants confused aspects of *need* which were routinely taken account of by the points scheme – the sharing, overcrowding and lack of amenity – with the relevant issue, i.e. that they were being told to leave. In most cases involving landlords' pressure, tenants relented and found their own alternative accommodation rather than negotiating for the necessary proof that made their homelessness 'actionable'. The advice centre workers in fact became convinced that officers in the housing department were fortunate not to have *more* homeless families coming to them than actually was the case.

Some other means of shortening the wait on the queue did exist in theory, but the workers encountered very few successes. Many applicants felt they had special medical need; typically, however, the extra points priority awarded for health reasons failed to bring about the immediate offer that they hoped for, and expected, and this served to convince many that officers in the housing department were ignoring their needs.

It was also discovered that there was a special social service/housing department liaison channel for dealing with special cases of 'social need'. But it was found that possibilities of an out-of-turn offer were only possible in cases where social workers had been involved for some considerable time, and this was the case for only very few of the enquirers. The local office of the social services department seemed unwilling to take on new cases – certainly not those defined to be experiencing only 'housing problems', and certainly not simply in order that use could be made of this special liaison scheme.

'Dispersal Policy'

Towards the end of their involvement, the advice centre workers became aware of a further aspect of the complexity. For some time they had been aware of a 'dispersal policy' operated by the housing department for its black tenants. They had never been sure how the policy worked. Certainly it was never mentioned by clerks over the telephone or in letters when particular cases were being discussed. Officially it was sometimes denied. One source declared that 'it is the policy of the Department that no distinction or differentiation is given in the housing of [Commonwealth] immigrants' (Birmingham Housing Department, untitled and undated brochure, *circa* 1972). Unofficially, however, the adviser heard of reference to ratios of black/white balance on landings in blocks of flats for streets and estates, and of a system of marking keys as vacancies occurred to ensure the maintenance of this balance. It should be apparent that in the context of area of choice this factor could quite simply be discriminatory. Also, given the complexity of the queue and grading system, it would be difficult to disentangle the consequences of such a policy from other aspects of allocation policy.

In 1975, the Race Relations Board considered Birmingham's scheme or policy of dispersal and found that the housing department had given 'unfavourable treatment' in offers to a particular family known to the advice centre workers. The housing department and the Race Relations Board disputed the rights and wrongs of the declared policy but in the end the department was forced to agree to disband its dispersal scheme.

Discretion

If the formal rules were not complex enough, then there was in addition the capacity referred to by the chairman of the housing committee when refuting queue-jumping that the system had a flexibility which enabled each case to be treated on its merits. Such flexibility, it is to be supposed, explained the frequency with which applicants were able to cite other families not having to wait so long, got a good house, or moved into a desired area, or the 'surprising' outcome on occasions for families who 'ought' to have had to wait a long time but were called sooner rather than later. Thus for most applicants this complex structure of rules was not fixed; it allowed for pressure, favours and special pleadings. It tended to underline the personalised and in-dividualistic nature of the wait in the queue.

The Response to Queueing

The long wait bred particular attitudes, as did the eventual arrival of an offer, especially when the offer was one that had to be refused because of type, location, cost, or an interplay of such factors. We can note some important common elements. One was the wish by many to interpret any sign or hint from the housing department in extremely positive terms. Applicants did write to and visit the department. If letters frequently went unanswered, visits at least achieved personalised contact with someone. By all accounts such contacts were brief; the clerk might note the request, look into the situation, and if there was something then the applicant would be notified. In this sort of exchange applicants tended to listen for positive hints. If the clerk said that no offer could be made *at least until* the visitor had been, people left convinced that they had been told that they would get an offer *when* they had had a visitor. If they were told that no offer could be made *at least until* they had spent a year on the waiting list, then this meant they would get an offer *when* their year's wait was over. Applicants shared some ambivalent feelings about these interviews. On one hand, it hardly seemed worth going to them: they did not seem to achieve anything; they had just been fobbed off by a junior clerk who 'didn't understand' or who seemed powerless or unwilling to do anything. At the same time there were nagging doubts that unless they persisted they would be forgotten.

It was a system which brought out competitive feelings since it

appeared that it was relativity of real need as much as formal position in
the queue which mattered. The greater importance of people's own
need relative to others had to be stressed. Their desert – their long
residence, clean rent record or long and regular employment – were
the grounds for their being given a house. Others, who had registered
recently, long after they had become eligible perhaps, had to claim that
those were the grounds for early consideration – they had not troubled
the council before and it was only right that they should be helped *now*
in their time of need.

The adviser, during home visits, would often ask people how they
thought the housing department worked and how they chose whom to
help. Most declared that they did not know: it was all incomprehensible; there was no system; it was just luck. Others had firmer
ideas: 'they' only helped white people, or alternatively 'they' never
helped white people, only if you were black. A few talked of people like
themselves who were consistently being denied help – the council was
not doing enough in their particular area. 'They' wanted to keep
everyone in the area – in the slums and not let them move out to nicer
areas. 'They' were prejudiced against black families or people who were
'low class'. About the most articulate expression of this sort of account
came from a Jamaican man:

> Well, to me, it's like this. These blokes [officers in the housing
> department] who hold these positions, they must be all right because
> they're not complaining. They are in what you call a high society and
> we who are in the low society suffer more. If we were in the high
> society, then they would help us straight away. But being as we are
> the low-class people then they don't want to know.

However, it was rare to find an awareness that discrimination and
unwillingness to help was general rather than specific to individual
cases. Most thought that the department *could* help them; they *were*
helping others like them; but someone, somewhere in the housing
department, had deliberately chosen not to assist. They *could* help, but
would not.

The comments of one middle aged woman were typical: 'They are
not bothering with us. It's useless. . . . I saw all those houses and flats
being built down the road. I was waiting all that time while they built
them but they did not offer me one, not one of them.'

The apparent discrimination was typified in the minds of many enquirers by what happened during their interviews at the housing department. As one young English mother put it:

> They just don't want to know. And the thing that gets me mad is, when I go up there [to the housing department], you get girls about seventeen and nineteen and they say it's not that bad and you look at them and you say 'Well, how do you know? You are living at home with your parents.' Most of them aren't married and they talk to you as if they know everything and you don't. You start getting mad at them and they say 'Well, that's it, we can't do anything for you.' And when you get the older people they go on about how it was 'worse in my day'.

Or, a Jamaican man:

> I go down there often. They just write on a bit of paper and send it upstairs, but sometimes I don't think it goes further than downstairs. They are not interested. As you go in they want to get rid of you. They haven't got any time for you really. Sometimes you get a good one that will sit down with you. Once I got a good one – she phoned upstairs and everything, she tried to help you. The rest of them can't be bothered with you.

Whatever explanation the enquirers gave of the system and why they were not getting help from it, all were aware of their powerless position. 'They', the housing department, decided whom they housed. All you could do was to plead and beg with them. As one West Indian man put it: 'I'm in no position to do anything. I depend on them. *They* are the ones who can help *me*. *I* can't help *them*.'

People were at the mercy of what 'they' thought. When the visitor called, as another West Indian man said: 'If she goes back and says we don't need a house then she keeps you back. It's what the visitor takes back, they have to go by that. If she says we can't keep a house (properly) then they put a ban on it.'

Two further themes recurred many times during conversations with enquirers. The first would be expressed like this: 'I have a friend who applied years after me and they gave them a house two years ago and I am still waiting!' Sometimes these apparent injustices could be seen in the light of the complexity of the situation – perhaps they had more points or they had widened their 'area of choice'. This type of explanation was part of housing advice. But, just as frequently, no account could be given and the workers had to confess themselves as mystified as their enquirers. The second complaint related to the way council properties – typically in the enquirers' areas of choice – appeared to stand empty for several months. Often they could not specify the exact location nor the length of time involved but the complaint recurred again and again. Both of these common complaints were a part of the knowledge of many enquirers that they were being ignored by the department and that those responsible for the queue were operating it unfairly.

Many wanted the advice centre workers to help them, holding great store by their efforts and were pleased when they promised to write to or ring the council on their behalf. Often enquirers told the adviser that they were relying on him for help.

With increasing certainty during the period of his involvement, the adviser shared little of such optimism. Neither the clerks he spoke to on the telephone, nor the officers to whom he wrote, had much control over events. Details of points, 'area of choice' and grading could be relayed, but nothing could be said about the likelihood of offers. Sometimes visits could be urged and promised; perhaps they came sooner than would have been the case had he not intervened. Very rarely did he or his colleagues try to urge the officers to make immediate offers or to give special consideration, as there appeared little difference between the needs of their many enquirers. To advocate the case of one would, to be consistent, have meant the advocacy of several hundred others. Occasionally there was an apparent misinterpretation of the rules of eligibility – unfair disadvantage could be corrected. At other times the workers would advocate consideration for certain families to be treated as 'actionably homeless' and to argue over the type of offer that would be made to families once homelessness had been established. Mostly, however, it was a case of ensuring that their enquirers were on the list, that their papers were in the right office, that all circumstances were recorded and that everything possible was known about the case and whether there was anything that the workers could get their enquirers to do to speed their progress to an offer. The atmosphere was mostly that of 'polite consultation'. After all, it was not really the fault of the clerks in the applications section of the housing department that there were not more properties available.

Housing Advice and Housing Associations:
What Alternatives?

Our view of management, allocation and of the response of those in housing need to the complex apparatus, whose simplified and 'visible' form was the 'queue', derives from the many interviews, consultations, telephone conversations, home visits and exchange of letters, all of which comprise housing advice. Somewhat ironically it was the case that the experience provided in addition a more direct insight into the workings and effects of the queue.

The establishment of the housing advice centre was intended to rationalise the housing association's process of tenant selection while trying to ensure that something was done for those for whom the chance of an association flat was as remote as that of a council house for many general applicants. Most of those who called at the advice centre were directed there from the association's office or knew of the link between the association and the advice centre. Many came expecting to be able to sign on a waiting list. However, the association was in a position to make some lettings, and particularly in its second and third years the advisers found themselves increasingly pressed to explain and justify their rationale for tenant selection. This experience provided further insight into the mechanisms of the queue administered by the council's housing department, for the advisers and the housing association, despite their hopes and wishes to provide an alternative means of access to decent housing, found themselves doing something rather similar.

Like the council, the association was disappointed in the rate at which it could produce additional units of accommodation for letting; like the council the association found itself unable to produce a balanced number of units of different sizes; the subsidy structure meant that one-bedroom units were in relative abundance but larger family accommodation was especially scarce. The most numerous and most needy of applicants were in search of the latter. The association sought to manage emergencies by provision of a hostel. In practice this supposedly 'temporary' provision became permanent unless a permanent tenancy was allocated and if that did occur then the association found out about 'queue-jumping'.

Where the advisers found they could be different was in the manner in which they sought to explain both the council and the association's methods of managing scarcity. Certainly they made efforts to create a friendly, informal atmosphere in which the circumstances of each case could be discussed. Furthermore, the workers tried, but only partially succeeded, in describing and explaining the complexity of the situation. It was not just a case of discrimination. There *was* a hope of a flat – eventually. It just meant playing the system properly – improving 'housekeeping standards' to get regraded, persuading a visitor to come round to make the application up to date, persuading the landlord to evict legally and therefore 'demonstrably', widening the 'area of choice', sometimes making a 'special case' for someone and then finally just waiting for an offer. There were also individual rights that could be secured – rent allowances, welfare benefits, rents that could be reduced and landlords who needed to be forced to do repairs.

The contradiction facing the adviser was that in order to demystify the system and show how individuals could take advantage of it meant, in the first instance, making it even more complex! It is hardly surprising, under those circumstances, that success in making the system more clear was, at best, partial. Furthermore, he and his colleagues re-emphasised an individualistic perspective on access: housing was a right but to get it you had to wait in the queue. All you could do was to play the game and perhaps shorten the waiting time. Some followed the advice, but when it failed to produce an immediate offer, resorted to their old conviction that they stood little chance of help. Others were more persistent and kept trying – since they had done everything they could, they might as well follow the adviser's counsel; it may work, one never knew. Some knew all the rules of the game before they came to the advice centre and the adviser was unable to suggest any further moves to them, save perhaps offer the distant hope of a place in some queue for a housing association flat if all else failed.

Sometimes the adviser would try to give more general explanations about the housing problem – why individuals had to wait so long was because not enough council houses were being built and this was because inadequate resources were available and because central government so often appeared to have priorities elsewhere. But even these attempts to place individual problems within their political context often failed; for attempts to *explain* and *account for* the shortage sounded, to many enquirers, just like the accounts, seen as excuses, offered by the officers and clerks in the housing department who had so often been heard to say things that sounded so similar – there were not enough properties and too many people wanting them. *Explaining* the shortage sounded the same as merely telling people that it existed and, anyway, as we have argued earlier, the apparent injustices of the queue tended to reduce the justification of any attempts to explain why that queue existed.

At all times, and in most cases, there was a tension and contradiction between *advice-giving* and deciding who should become a tenant of the local housing association, and when. Many people came with expectations concerning the latter – they wanted a flat from the workers and wanted to present their case. The workers usually would not, and more frequently *could not*, provide one, at least in the short term; all they could do was to give advice and less immediate help. With an extremely long waiting list and a declining number of new association properties, the advice centre could only organise applicants into queues and try and see that basic housing rights were exercised during the waiting period. For both the adviser and the applicants there was so often a sense of futility. All possibilities had been tried and there was to be no release from the cramped room or temporary and nerve-shattering lodging with increasingly impatient relatives or friends – at least not for a while. Sometimes all the adviser could do was to encourage the enquirers in their search for a private room or two, give them a list of estate agents and advise them not to worry too much about the rent – there were always rent allowances, the rent tribunal, or rent officer. Occasionally he could offer the address of a room rumoured to be vacant, or a landlord who owned several houses – a token effort and one which rarely succeeded in securing someone a room. These enquirers were essentially on their own in their search – something they were quite used to and which most had been used to for many years. All the adviser had done was to promise, and perhaps make more likely, a decent place in the future; but for the next few months, if not years, there was not much chance, or hope, of anything better.

Access to Council Housing: Housing Class and Urban Management

We found it hard to discern in all this complexity any shared access to the 'means of housing'; nor was there much sense of a market or power relationship between these applicants and those who were providers. Yet in other ways we could not fail to be struck by many broad similarities in the position and circumstances of the applicants. Almost every enquirer was a worker, either unskilled or skilled, whether or not employed. For those who were in work, wages were either below or around the national average. Although some appeared to be at a stage in the family/earnings cycle which would eventually pass, leading to an increase in their market power to obtain decent housing, for many more no such change seemed likely. They were dependent upon state provision and the chances are that what the state provided was unlikely to be desirable in a number of respects. There seems to be no sense or value in the idea of there being here a number of *housing classes* – here was a sector of the working class whose power relative to housing seemed a reflection of their position relative to the means of production: what they earned limited their scope and there was no discernable 'independence' of their class position, so defined from their position in the housing market.

Moreover, it was difficult to discern in the relationship between the managers and the managed any sense of mediation or representation of interests. The allocation of council houses was determined not by the managers but by the scarcity of housing as a market commodity. That objective fact explains the nature of the managerial style adopted both by housing department officials and by the housing advisers. Variations in manner, in the time spent and the sort of conversations adopted could not conceal a similar purpose: to induce patience among those waiting, to proffer some hope of eventual gain relating to the maintenance of an orderly queue.

Until enough houses were built, housing conditions for a substantial section of the local population were extremely poor and with little prospect of improvement. There was, however, very little protest, certainly no protest about the collective, unfulfilled needs of the urban poor in our area. People only protested about their case and how they, individually, were being overlooked. The queue, the complexities of access, perceived injustices and lack of explanation effectively divided the interests of this section of the urban working class and obscured any shared interests that may have existed had circumstances been different.

The housing situation of the poor was communicated as one of individualised need; and whether those in need turned to the council, to a housing association, or to the advice centre, they had this position of individual need confirmed and underlined. The processes of these organisations administered and legitimised queueing for a decent house. For the efforts and activities with which we were involved, we can make no other claim.

Chapter 4

Case Study 2: Residents' Action in a Redevelopment Area

Redevelopment: Birmingham – the Context

In the last chapter we noted that one aspect of the 'plight' of ordinary applicants on the waiting list for council houses appeared to be their relative low priority for available lettings, the cream of which in number and quality went to those families affected by comprehensive redevelopment and slum clearance. We also noted that in our period of study there was a slump in new council building over demolitions so the relative position of ordinary applicants worsened.

Our second case study explores the position of this apparently privileged group: residents in a redevelopment area currently experiencing clearance.

It is perhaps valuable to remind the reader of the size and scope of Birmingham's post-war redevelopment. Birmingham city council took full advantage of wartime legislation to acquire large tracts of poor-quality, inner-city housing for eventual comprehensive redevelopment. The acquisition and planning of five comprehensive development areas was the city's major post-war concern, and the work of rehousing families and new building got underway in the early 1950s. In 1955 a second phase of comprehensive redevelopment was planned in outline and a number of areas outside the original five C.D.A.s labelled for eventual treatment. The rate of progress in the five C.D.A.s was highly satisfactory and by 1970 work on the second phase was underway. Up to 1970 the council had cleared some 45,000 unfit houses – 25,000 in the C.D.A.s and the remainder through Housing Act powers in the second phase areas. At that time some 20,000 further homes awaited clearance or acquisition in these areas and 1976 was the target year for fulfilment of the whole undertaking.

The Area

The case study area is one such area – about a mile from a city centre towards the south, and lying between a main road, a railway line and part of the city's main, but yet to be constructed, middle ring road. When built and until about 1950 it comprised some 1500 houses, packed close in terraces, some fronting the road, others at the rear. A few were a bit larger than the rest and had small front gardens. Small workshops and yards, corner shops, a surprising number of pubs, and the proximity of the railway line and its terminal goods yards, all testified to its original purpose. Here were plain houses for working men. Whatever qualities they possessed in the nineteenth century, few remained to justify their survival into the second half of the twentieth century, certainly not in the view of the planners, officers and leaders of the city council.

By 1971, when our research interest commenced, it was a muddle and chaos which, with seeming inevitability, typifies local-authority redevelopment in progress: old houses (some derelict, some lived in, some closed and bricked up), new houses, houses being built, houses being knocked down, odd workshops and yards, several pubs in various states of dilapidation, corner stores, the occasional shop-fronted house, two schools, an elegant church facing the main road, used-car lots and filling stations on the middle ring.

In 1971 a survey carried out by the local community association discovered about 850 houses: 107 were empty, 585 were inhabited but due for demolition by 1975, 93 were old houses that were not going to be cleared, and 65 were council houses of recent construction.

About 1500 people were living in the houses due for clearance: nearly 40 per cent of heads of households were elderly if not actually of pensionable age; nearly 40 per cent had lived at their present address for more than twenty years; more than half were of just one or two persons and about half were born in Birmingham; 52 per cent lived in privately rented unfurnished accommodation and more than half of the houses had no bathroom and only outside lavatories. In some ways, therefore, the area corresponded with a common stereotype of redevelopment areas: an area of much private renting and elderly, long-standing residents for whom the planned upheaval was likely to be a major and catastrophic turn of events.

The survey, however, also revealed considerable heterogeneity. There were a number of large families with relatives nearby and who were long-term residents of the area; most were of Asian origin. There were also a number of single-parent families, often in furnished rooms or in an old council house. Many single working people, unmarried couples, groups of friends and elderly residents all contributed to the diversity of the area. The immigrants were fairly evenly distributed between those from other parts of the British Isles, Ireland, Asia and the Caribbean. Most of these were young families and relative newcomers to the area rather than having been born in Birmingham. They also were more likely to be owners of their own houses rather than tenants.

When the survey was made the council already owned about 10 per cent of the occupied houses and most of the other residents were waiting for the council takeover: 30 per cent were owners and about 6 per cent were tenants in furnished accommodation who typically occupied one or two rooms in a house shared with its owner; 70 per cent of all working residents had less than three miles to travel to their work-place and 50 per cent worked in the immediate vicinity.

The Plan

Planning the redevelopment of an area is a long and complex process. In Birmingham the structure of local government has done nothing to reduce this complexity. The several departments involved have no history of a corporate or co-ordinated approach. The planning and redevelopment section of the *public works department* was responsible for over-all planning in the area which had been designated in 1955 as one in which comprehensive redevelopment would occur. The evidence for such a decision came from reports of the housing inspectors of the *public health department* on areas of unfitness. Since 1957 the making of such reports has been a duty of a local authority under the terms of the 1957

Housing Act. It was the *housing department* which actually made decisions about the number, size, whereabouts and timing of clearance areas: a specialised section of the department piloted housing compulsory-purchase orders through their various phases. If there was a public enquiry, the notices and information derived from the *town clerk's department*. Other specialised sections of the housing department dealt with the *management* of acquired houses until demolition and the *rehousing* of residents. Actual demolition work was authorised by the *public works department*. Negotiations with owners and tenants about compensation, well-maintained payments, home-loss payments and the like were the work of the *city estates department*.

Demolition work in the area had started in the early 1960s and was to continue beyond 1975. From 1970 about twelve clearance areas of housing compulsory-purchase orders were made within the terms of the 1957 Housing Act. Although such compulsory powers allow a local authority to acquire all the land within a clearance area and may include fit houses and other property and/or adjoining land to make clearance areas of a regular shape and size viable for redevelopment, only very few of the shops, workshops, factories and yards were included in these areas. These, and some odd patches of mainly fit houses, were included in a later and larger compulsory-purchase order within the powers afforded local authorities by the 1971 Town and Country Planning Act. The detailed organisation of this Order involved the planning and redevelopment section of the *public works department* and the *city estates department*.

Detailed redevelopment proposals were presented by the chief planning officer to the *public works committee* in April 1971. A map indicated proposed land use – housing, shops, public open spaces – and showed that some housing was not to be affected by acquisition and clearance proposals.

A second map indicated which blocks of houses were to be cleared in which year 'subject to acquisition' – a sort of declaration of demolition intent; 1972 and 1974 were to be the main years of demolition.

The report provided an explanation of the proposals, some indication of the number and size of new houses to be built, and it also stated:

> The redevelopment of parts [of the area] before redevelopment in other parts of the area should make it possible to provide accom-modation, prior to the demolition of their existing homes, for those people who wish to remain in the area, either because of family ties or

for other reasons. Special attention should also be paid to the provision of accommodation for those persons who work in the area.

This belief in, and hope for, a *phased* redevelopment, so that people who wanted could remain in the area in new houses, was stressed at two public meetings for local residents. The first of these took place in April 1971 but only about six residents from our area were present. No doubt many more would have come had more and better publicity been given. A few weeks later a further meeting was organised involving a different approach; a brief statement from a council member was followed by individual counselling by officers from the planning section; some 100 residents learned of the proposals in this way.

The nature of the hoped-for phasing will be explained in some detail, but it should be noted that these proposals were but the latest in a series. We have not been able to discover any earlier public meetings to explain proposals, but in important respects the new proposals contained an extension of redevelopment and showed a change of emphasis in priorities from plans made three years earlier.

Plans for substantial clearance and rebuilding were made first in the mid-1960s but at that time the area was considered for planning purposes as part of a larger area including some streets of houses which, despite multi-occupation and overcrowding, were technically fit within the terms of the Housing Act. The proposal to demolish those houses provoked great controversy – many of the occupants were relative newcomers to the city and many were from Asia and the Caribbean. The proposals were shelved.

In 1967 revised proposals again deferred action on the mulit-occupied houses and proposed selective demolition and rebuilding in our area; certain roads of old terraced housing were designated for retention and qualified for improvement-grant aid. A feature of these proposals was for a small area to be made a public open space and some cleared land in the northern part was subsequently transferred from the housing department to the public works department for this purpose. Between 1967 and 1970 clearance consistent with these plans continued and some new building commenced. We would estimate that about twenty homes in the 'retained' streets were improved with grant aid and houses were bought and sold for prices of about £2000 during this period.

The reasons for the changes from these plans are not clear. The 1971 chief officer's report simply stated:

Since [the 1967] layout was approved, certain changes have taken place within the area which detract from the approved layout. It was originally anticipated that a large proportion of the properties would be worthy of retention. However, since that time a number of the houses have been included in clearance areas and all but a few properties are under review by the Chief Public Health and Housing Inspector with a view to further clearance action.

The new proposals relocated and enlarged the area of public open space; this was explained in terms of serving needs of the whole of the 'action area', of which these latest proposals were but a part. The new area of open space included not only the most substantial area already cleared but also those streets formerly 'retained'. The previously designated public open space was redesignated for housing and transferred back to the relevant department. Finally, a block of houses included in earlier proposals for demolition were placed in a 'retained' category.

No officer at the public meetings was able to say when particular parts of the area would be affected. In this respect, and from the viewpoint of the residents, there was no change. This uncertainty in detail remained a problem for most of the residents who came to the various meetings, small or large, formal or informal, that occurred over the next few years. No officer could point to a programme or time-table, and, if pressed, would have to concede that there were so many uncertainties, so many departments and authorities involved that it was not possible to be precise.

The first public meetings were organised by the planners, and the resolutions which were the basis for these meetings had been passed by the public works committee. However, it became clear that the planners and the committee making these proposals did not have powers to implement the plans. The actual rate of acquisition was determined by the public health department and the housing department and the rate of rehousing and the actual lay-out and timing of new building was a matter for the housing department and housing committee. The status of these proposals was therefore not quite as it seemed to be at the public meetings. One item clearly within the powers of the public works department – the making of a *planning* compulsory-purchase order for industrial and commercial premises and remaining 'fit' houses – was not mentioned at these meetings, yet the commencement of much demolition and rebuilding was dependent on such an order being completed. That did not occur until 1975.

Most residents greeted the proposals with a certain scepticism based on many years of experiencing similar proposals but no action. For them the plans were perhaps a sign of hope but they were certainly not something on which to pin too much faith or on which to base any plans or action about moving house.

Research – Action: Work with the Residents' Action Group

One member of the audience at the first public meeting in 1971 was a community worker with a voluntary organisation involved in a varied community and social-work undertaking in the neighbourhood of which the redevelopment area was a part. He was impressed by the organisation of a residents' association in an adjoining area and was interested in the proposals for 'phasing'. Through another community worker he contacted the research team for assistance with a household survey whereby the scope and potential both for a residents' association and for 'phasing' might be discovered. Subsequently he and other members of his organisation were willing to have one of the researchers join a group interested in providing advice and assistance to individuals and to a residents' association if one was formed.

This small group – the community worker, a local churchman, an elderly voluntary helper, a director of a housing association – being familiar with the consequences of large-scale redevelopment in other areas of the city, subscribed to a view that the attendant 'break up of community' carried severe social costs with it, and so were positively interested in this 'phasing' whereby the benefits of redevelopment might be obtained without these anti-community costs. None were experienced in work with groups of residents or with community action. All would have been sceptical about the city council's capacity to take care of the human issues of redevelopment.

The survey was carried out in June – July 1971. Hurried organisation, inexperienced questioners and over-complex schedules meant that the information was patchy and uncertain. However, for the more important items a reasonable response rate was obtained. Over-all contact was with 380 of 478 households. The agreed aim was to use the information gained for contact with individuals and for a public meeting at which the idea of a residents' association could be discussed.

In the summer, however, the community worker left the neighbourhood organisation. The member of the research team was appointed to the job on a basis that allowed continuing involvement in the research project. The job involved other duties, and changes within the organisation meant that the small group which initiated the project in the redevelopment area no longer met and this aspect of the organisation's work became the sole responsibility of the researcher/community worker.

He had attended discussions with the group and disagreed with none of their assumptions. He was familiar with reports from other cities about slum clearance and was familiar with the visible outcomes of Birmingham's plans. His familiarity with some of the sociological literature on 'community' made him cautious in attributing too much of its 'break-up' to redevelopment. He had no direct experience of community action but was familiar with a number of other moves in the city to improve or effect 'participation'. Without supposing that residents' action would drastically alter the situation, he saw gains for the local people and supposed others might accrue to 'the managers' if there was a concerted attempt to provide information about, and co-ordinate the operation of, policy. That something could and should be attempted in the area was underlined by the students who carried out the surveys. They had reported appalling conditions, great uncertainty and some considerable hostility from people, many of whom said they would like to stay in the area if it was redeveloped.

Other student helpers attached to the neighbourhood organisation visited homes in the area and delivered leaflets about a public meeting set for November. Some 200 persons attended. The researcher, as community worker with the neighbourhood organisation, addressed the meeting, giving some information gained from the survey. He stressed that there seemed to be many unanswered questions and uncertainties which a residents' association could answer. A worker from the adjoining area spoke briefly and effectively about how the residents' association worked in his area.

What was being recommended was a form of organisation and style of action which benefited from assistance given by community workers and researchers and other 'professionals' or 'outsiders' but which was directed by, and identified with, local people. There was quite lively and prolonged discussion, rather more about the conditions in the area, requests for information and protest than about forming an association, but when people were invited to provide names to form a committee about thirty people did so. The following week this group met, elected officers and set about organising their first meeting – with their local councillors.

For the next two years the group met regularly and organised a number of meetings and events. It was assisted by a student helper from the neighbourhood organisation and the community worker who attended most of its meetings, had contact with its members, joined in other events and in a general manner became involved in its operations. That involvement has provided access to most of the information upon which this case study is based. Things were 'found out' with or on behalf of this residents' group'

A second form of involvement and way of 'finding out' derived from the provision of housing advice. The community worker's job entailed responsibility for a weekly advice bureau on housing matters in the wider neighbourhood; this service was expanded in 1973 when a shop-front advice centre was opened. The role of housing adviser was dealt with at some length in the previous case study; it allows for considerable contact with departments of the local authority and contact for varying lengths of time with those being advised. Over the course of two years some 100 people from the redevelopment area were given advice. A group of these were visited in their homes and provided a large amount of information on which this study will draw.

The action group, with some changes in membership, met regularly until November 1973. Apart from ordinary meetings, two public meetings were held under its auspices as well as several smaller meetings with certain city officials: petitions and newsletters were circulated; two information surveys were conducted by members; outings, jumble-sales and raffles were organised. It would be wrong to say that the action group achieved a representative membership; indeed one of its major concerns was how to involve more people on a regular basis. Its true membership in terms of those who attended regularly and took an active part in its organisation and direction was never more than ten people. The number of people who attended a few meetings and then came no more was very considerable, perhaps a hundred; and the number of people reached by its meetings, newsletters, enquiries and the like was greater still.

However, the style of its operation ensured that it reflected wide and diverse opinions and, through its activities at different stages, that it came in contact with the many themes and issues of the redevelopment process. Its work and efforts went through a number of phases which reflected different interests. Initially it tackled the question of 'phasing' and sought to organise a lobby of those committed to staying in the area and in the new houses. A petition was sent to the director of housing by those wanting local rehousing. Support for this waned, however, once an informal survey revealed a mixed state of feelings about the issue and an unwillingness on the part of most to actually come to action group meetings to state their case. Delays in the building of new council houses in the area meant that the housing department could not agree to the group's suggestion that a special waiting list be kept for the local new houses and the enthusiasts for 'phasing' became disillusioned and rapidly isolated.

The second phase of residents' action concerned conditions in the area and the interests of those who were not going to be moved soon but who were going to be left until last or whose houses were not going to be demolished. As it became clearer to the action group's regular members through information from one of the local councillors and the community worker that new building was going to be delayed, the purpose of the group became more and more a channel of complaints about conditions in the area. The councillor encouraged them in this. Members found their neighbours remarkably uncommunicative about such matters and again it was left to a few to find out and complain. Perhaps understandably a few people actually joined in order to complain but a small group spent a lot of time visiting old people, doing some boarding-up and leak-stopping, and became known as people who would make the necessary representations to the relevant department.

Throughout its life the action group kept in close touch with one of the local councillors. Identifying himself more with a group of elderly white residents, he provided encouragement to the group, exhorting it not to give up but to continue its struggle. He was not a member of a relevant committee of the council involved in the redevelopment process, and as such there was a difference between his role as decision-maker on the council and his role of local councillor. In many ways he played the role of local councillor very well. He regularly attended group meetings and took up the cases of many individuals with the relevant department. Like the other councillors and council officials he was seen at the end of each public meeting busily writing down the names and addresses of those who had some complaint.

Towards the end of its active life the main purpose of the action group became that of finding ways of speeding up the whole process, both the demolition and the rebuilding. What could be done? Who would be left behind until last? The group declined in size and in frequency of meetings as the clearance programme got under way. Almost its last meeting was with a senior housing department official who was able to give some stark and plain information: to move quickly meant taking what was offered. The housing visitors had called and the necessary information was collected. It was now simply a matter of time. People in this situation did not really need a residents' association to help them wait. Eventually the group stopped meeting. The chairman was having a private argument with the housing department about an offer in an area of his choice. The community worker and one of the members who lived in one of the recently built council houses tried to organise a meeting for the new residents to carry on the struggle for better conditions, but there was insufficient interest shown and the action group wound up its affairs.

Redevelopment: the Process Examined

On Phasing

The plans presented in November 1971 appeared to promise some definite progress, to suggest a time-table, and to allow for 'phasing'. It may have been clear to residents at the public meetings that it would not, or could not, work, that things could not go as smoothly as the council were making out and that there would be no early release from the years of uncertainty, dirt and gradual deterioration. If this had not been clear to residents at that time, it rapidly became clear for most of them during the months and years which followed.

The author of the chief officer's report was the then head of the planning and redevelopment section of the public works department. He was on the verge of retirement when the proposals were approved and subsequently discussed his intentions with the community association representatives, including the community worker. He was a man of somewhat eccentric manner, entertaining and enthusiastic and a thoroughgoing *aficionado* of the participatory craze since he was quite sure that *his* ideas, tiresome to the straight planning bureaucrats, were of immediate appeal to ordinary people. In putting in the idea of 'phasing' the redevelopment, so that those residents who wished to stay could do so, he felt sure he was reflecting both progressive thinking and residents' interests. It was not the case that the proposal was based on any survey or test of opinion; indeed that was true of the whole operation. There was only a cursory inspection of exteriors. The proposed number and mix of new building was not based on any knowledge of the nature of the local community. Indeed it was a standard mix when, as we have suggested, the social structure of the area was extremely heterogeneous. So the proposition for 'phasing' was based on an assumption that it was what people wanted. In part the assumption rested on the belief that people who had put down roots resisted the upset and reorientation involved. It also recognised that such inner-city areas had advantages and attractions for those whose work-place was near by. Preventing the 'break-up of the community' was the most commonly used expression to justify this 'phasing'.

At various stages, different attempts were made by the community association and action group to find out what local people wanted. The initial survey asked respondents: 'When demolition happens, what would you prefer . . . to stay in this area, to stay near by, or to move away?' About 60 per cent stated a preference for staying, 35 per cent for moving away, the rest being undecided. When set against information about age, length of stay and work-place, it became apparent that there was no simple division between the elderly wanting to stay and newcomer families wanting to go. Indeed, if anything, contrary to stereotype, it was those who had recently arrived who were more likely to prefer to stay.

However, it was clear that the question was somewhat abstract for many respondents: When was demolition going to occur? *Was* demolition going to occur? What alternative would be available? What would happen in the meantime? What would rents be in any new houses to be built? All these queries were directly relevant but, at the time of enquiry, unanswerable.

Later the residents' action group made a further enquiry when they were informed that 'starts' on over a hundred houses were due shortly. Although this enquiry was not as systematic in coverage as the other survey, it had the advantage of being a simple self-survey, asking respondents to name areas of choice if they wished to move and the form provided indicated clearly where the new houses would be. A similar sort of response was obtained. More than half preferred to stay but by no means all of them were small elderly white households. Following this enquiry a small group of seventeen families addressed a petition to the director of housing saying they wished to stay.

Those willing to express so definite a choice were few. Most people were more cautious: it did not seem to them that the housing department actually gave people much choice so it was perhaps unwise to get worked up and fixed on somewhere or something that might not happen; 'let's wait and see' was the more usual attitude.

In fact the 'starts' on the new building were severely delayed and painfully slow for any who had high hopes. Moreover, the housing department changed the clearance programme and included in an earlier phase several rows of houses where originally clearance might have occurred after some rebuilding. This change was called 'accelerated clearance'. It meant that families started to be moved out a year earlier than had been proposed. This incident revealed that the council's clearance date more correctly meant 'the year in which the housing department will start to move families out so that houses can be demolished'. It goes without saying that this acceleration was not discussed with the residents. All it meant was the visitors from the housing departments started 'visiting' sooner than residents expected. Many people were very pleased at this. More ambivalent feelings were expressed by some of those who had signed the petition to the director of housing. The housing visitors could not tell them when the new houses would be finished, nor could they say that they could be allocated one now for certain, nor even put on a list for consideration. Some families initially indicated they would wait but when neighbours' houses began to be emptied and the familiar pattern of vandalism, dossing and children's play started in the emptied homes, most relented and chose to leave. Among those to leave were the two most regular and enthusiastic supporters of the action group, those who had earlier been the most committed to a revival of the area in which they were born.

Despite the attempts to accelerate clearance in 1972, the over-all housing situation in the city meant that the clearance programme was slowed down in 1973 and 1974 by extreme shortages of suitable alternative property. A major factor in this was a slump in new council-house-building. Our area was directly affected and it was one of the first areas to benefit when, eventually, the situation eased.

Some of the complexities of housing allocation described in the previous chapter were also at work in our area. It was noticeable, for instance, that large families were particularly slow to be moved since the shortage of four- and five-bedroomed houses was especially extreme. Those graded for older or interwar housing had to wait longer for offers than those thought suitable for post-war houses and sometimes they were not aware of the adverse grading and why they were only offered unsuitable houses.

So, even if the idea or principle of 'phasing' had been grasped by a co-ordinated management team, it was likely that these broader constraints would have produced difficulties; without such co-ordination, 'phasing' was never a starter.

The planners' proposals, however, did to some extent come to pass. When, finally, new homes were completed there were still families wishing to move from houses in clearance areas and some of these families moved to new houses in the area. However, at no time would the housing department admit that any clearance families could have priority or first-call on the new homes. Each individual case was treated on its merits and the element of choice was crucial; if people from other areas chose our area that was as valid as someone choosing to stay in our area. Need, eligibility and area of choice were the main factors taken into account. So, although there are many from our area in the new houses, there are as many from other areas. Many of those for whom staying in the area would have been attractive did not, or could not, wait for the chance to stay. Staying, it seems, depended more on factors beyond the individual's control – the working out in the unco-ordinated way we have described of the several policies and practices whose totality is the process of redevelopment.

The planners' 'phasing' was thus an abstraction, a hope which bore little relation to actual conditions in the area.

On Choice

Very few people resented the fact that a development programme existed, but most resented the way in which it was carried out. When council officers came to public meetings with proposals, plans and maps, they could not answer queries about 'when' (someone else's job), 'where' (someone else's again), or about 'what would happen in the meantime'. The process whereby offers of alternative accommodation were made reinforced for many the feelings of helplessness, of a lack of choice, and of being pushed about.

The fragmentary and piecemeal process of acquisition meant that, for all residents, there was no direct relation between the date of takeover and the timing of a move. When the council took over management of a property, a visitor from the housing department would provide a rent book, explain about rents, rent collection and repairs, but would stress that this was nothing to do with getting rehoused. The letter sent to each tenant at that time gave a very clear message: 'don't call us, we'll call you'. However, some tenants who did try and move quickly found it was possible – particularly if they had been on the waiting list before acquisition and would accept an area where accommodation (probably a flat) was available. Others, for whom a special case could be made, perhaps with the support of a councillor and/or doctor, might also be moved. The routine practice, however, was that in the year set for clearance – and the residents' group tried to make this information widely known – a visitor would call and take certain information from the tenant. Through the process of providing housing advice we learned to realise the significance of this visit and it is something worth exploring in some detail.

The housing department claims that families in clearance areas are rehoused wherever possible in homes of a suitable size and in their area of choice. Its claim is that during the whole slum-clearance programme it has not been found necessary to evict a single family in order to get a site cleared.

The visiting housing officer provides the main and most significant point of personal contact between the housing department and its clients. Visitors, like so many local-government officials, have heavy work-loads, and are bound by quite firm rules and routines. In our area their visits tended to be short, almost cursory, and discussions with senior officials suggested why this was so. It was considered to be well known in areas like ours what people wanted; there was little or no need for extensive discussion about areas of choice as most people can be assumed to know the basic rules and so can be treated routinely. There is a great deal of justification for this view: in our experience most residents had been waiting for this visit and the move and were ready to go almost anywhere. Many had seen their neighbours move, had a good idea of the areas of the city in which old friends were now living, and so were clear about their idea of choice. All our evidence would suggest that once the visitors do call, and provided that the routine holds, all is well. As we have indicated, most of the concern in the area was about the living conditions and the timing of the move.

However, that is not the complete story. Not everyone fits into the routine and many of these families discovered that for them there was a long wait and considerable anxiety before a move came. Moreover, there were enough of these to convey to neighbours that all was not smooth and routine but that the housing department worked in mysterious and authoritarian ways and had rules and requirements which seemed to disregard individual choice. In a situation of uncertainty and anxiety, a few instances of harsh treatment can be far more significant as a source of rumour and as support of myth than the many routine and unexceptional cases. The way the visitors went about their work seemed to take little account of this background and context of uncertainty and anxiety, and any family with an unusual request could find themselves seemingly forgotten.

A particularly significant case concerned a middle-aged lady who shared her house with her brother. That in itself would make it non-routine, one might have thought. She asked the visitor whether she could be housed on her own since she did not get on well with her brother. She was told that the council could not offer both her and her brother separate accommodation. Nothing more was said. The resident was a shy and nervous lady who would find such contacts something of an ordeal. Soon after the families in neighbouring houses started to be moved and eventually just two or three families remained. The lady was visited a second time but this appears to have achieved nothing. Then demolition started until just her house was left in isolation. The lady's electricity and water supplies were severed for most of a weekend, it was mid-November, a time of cold winds which swept into the open roof space of her now isolated house. Through a neighbour on the opposite side of the street who was active in the action group, she came to the local advice centre and a telephone call to the housing department confirmed that the problem was that she was requesting separate housing for her brother. A discussion with the brother confirmed his willingness to move independently. He was simply waiting for his sister to be moved but did not want to leave her in that house on her own. In a relatively short time an offer of a small maisonette was made, which the lady accepted. Here was a clear case of officers in the housing department hoping that a problem would go away and making no effort to ease the situation. The lady was unable to help herself and was not actually sure what the housing department would do; she did not expect them simply to do nothing. But more important for our story is the impact such treatment had on neighbours, for it confirmed for many the callous and unfeeling way the housing department treated people.

A great many misunderstandings arise about the *size* of alternative homes that could be offered to small families. Many in our area were elderly and had brought up families in these houses. Their children and grandchildren used to come and stay, so many liked having a spare room. The relative spaciousness of the houses and their small gardens were advantages which offset the lack of modern amenities. Many hoped that they would be offered a small house and garden or at least a two-bedroomed ground-floor flat with a garden. Two-bedroomed houses and ground-floor flats were in very short supply and three-bedroomed accommodation was as scarce. So there was an understandable pressure on visitors to find prospective tenants for the many flats which the department possessed. These pressures and the making of offers of flats to people who had said they wanted houses gave rise to a belief that the council forced people to take flats. However, many people knew neighbours who had recently got a house and felt there was a difference between what the visitors said and what you actually got. In addition it became apparent that people who had been long-standing waiting-list applicants were favoured for houses, and some families who had owned their houses (and so had not been on the waiting list) feared that they would be harshly treated. This was something which seemed more a fear than a reality since it was rare to find people not moving for these reasons. There were common beliefs that if you insisted and showed no wavering you could get what you wanted *in the end*. There were also common beliefs that many people accepted the first place offered even if it was not ideal, since 'moving out' became top priority.

Pressure to move out, even to somewhere far from ideal, was also exerted by a widespread belief that families only received three offers and were then evicted. The element of truth in this was that after three offers were made and refused the case was routinely reviewed and if the offers had been of an appropriate size in the eyes of the department and in the resident's area of choice, then it would be referred to a special housing sub-committee who might ask to interview the resident, or, what seemed more usual, authorised the department to make a further offer prior to commencing proceedings for possession, i.e. sending a letter threatening a notice to quit. We learned of some cases where the matter was referred to the sub-committee and one instance where a letter was sent. In that case the family was subsequently offered precisely what they had asked for two years previously, for which they had constantly been informed they were not eligible, and told that such properties were in extremely short supply.

Whether at public meetings, group meetings, or at individual advice sessions, a recurring theme was whether 'choice' was a real factor. When a senior official from the department told a group that 'you won't be pushed about, we know that, we try and rehouse you where you want', polite disbelief greeted his assurance. That was not how it felt. It was of course the case that, whatever senior officials said, the visitors knew that to explain about areas of choice, numbers of offers, committee review rules and size was not very helpful to rehousing officers who only had accommodation of certain types and sizes to give. Also, they knew that the programme depended on what was available. As our experience of the area and the process grew, we saw that it became increasingly difficult for individual choices to be satisfied and for the rate of clearance to be maintained. Our view of the allocation system suggests that families in clearance areas, whatever they have suffered in the time up to acquisition and clearance, are in a relatively privileged position when it comes to rehousing and get some definite priority for properties that are available for letting by the housing department: in 1972–3 even that kind of privilege could not provide speedy and satisfactory rehousing.

Very few who came to the advice centre would believe this supposed priority status and in many instances they were people whose situation was not sufficiently routine to get a suitable offer immediately. But by and large it was clear that considerable effort and energy went into organising a supply of suitable houses in suitable areas for clearance-area families and most did get what they told the visitor they wanted, or accepted the first or second offer made to them.

By the end of our research period the rate of clearance had slowed down and those families who were remaining were not just those sticking out for something special or whose size of family or housekeeping standards were putting them at the back of the queue. In fact they were families who a few years before would have been moved long ago. Furthermore, the extent of 'privilege' was being questioned at policy level. The housing committee chairman was on record as suggesting that clearance-area families should expect to take a turn in a block of flats, and a quota of houses that might have been used to ease allocations in clearance areas was now to be used for transfers from high-rise blocks.

In our area, however, the pressure to accept flats, the lack of any feeling of privilege or priority, and the feeling of being pushed about, were part of the routine of redevelopment, and this was in part because of the way the housing visitor, the personalised contact whereby policy becomes practice, provided (and withheld) information.

Anxiety and uncertainty meant for many that a move, anywhere, was better than staying. Others, those who did stick it out, usually got what they wanted. So, from the viewpoint of the housing department, the policy of satisfying choice actually worked – people always moved without having to be evicted. It meant, then, that for the housing department the planners' notion of 'phasing' was irrelevant: choices could be met without it. Those residents who responded to the 'phasing' suggestion found that the department it most concerned, the housing department, was quite disinterested in their response; and their efforts to make phasing a reality led nowhere.

On Conditions in the Area

The physical conditions of the area were the overriding concern for most residents. Indeed this anxiety lay behind their worries about timing: how long would it be before clearance, and would things get better?

The most pervasive complaints related to the security of empty houses, the prevention of vandalism and the achievement of security. When the houses in our area were built, it was for a single owner to let to tenants. For reasons of economy and need, roof spaces were continuous and not walled between each house. When individual homes were sold off, the structure did not change. So it was possible to walk in the roof space from one end of the street to another. A major fear of residents when houses were vacated in a block was that burglaries would occur through these roof spaces. Whether in fact many burglaries did occur is immaterial, the fear was real. The action group tried to get assurances from the council that houses would be bricked up at the front and rear whenever it was clear that a house would be empty for a matter of months. Apart from one or two houses dealt with in this way, it never became routine.

The routine was that within a few days of being vacated council workmen would nail pieces of corrugated iron over doorways and windows. Often this was done before gas and electricity service men had removed fittings and fuses so they would have to tear off the iron sheets and break the door locks, usually failing to resecure them on departure. A worried neighbour would report the matter to the housing department. By this time the tatters would have visited to remove any lead or other saleable metal fittings. If, as was usual, this meant severing a water main, then the adjoining houses would find their water pressure severely reduced until the water leak was sealed. Depending on the time of year the house might become a place to doss down for tramps and/or an adventure playground for children. Acquisition was piecemeal, rehousing was piecemeal, demolition was piecemeal. For many families the consequences of these piecemeal operations lasted for ten years.

In each year houses were being cleared and sites of various sizes were becoming empty. Some buildings were vacated and knocked down while others remained unoccupied. Some remained occupied and became isolated for no clear reason. The site that was to have been a park became an overgrown tip and remained so until building started eight years after clearance. Sites attracted various uses: car and lorry parks, dumps and rubbish tips. Pavements, mostly of the old slate-brick sort, became crushed as vehicles crossed them to reach the open space – and remained broken and dangerous for the remaining population. The area became a tip and an eyesore. Occupied houses became hard to distinguish amidst the dereliction, and those residents who remembered how the area used to be found it difficult to recognise.

Many withdrew into the comfort and decency of their own homes, and those who were owner-occupiers, and some tenants, kept the houses decorated and spotless to the last, as if in some way compensating for the chaos beyond their front doors. Others were not so fortunate. Few landlords chose to spend more than a minimum to maintain the properties, and with acquisition being promised at some future date such action made economic sense when rents had remained low for years; but for tenants it meant months or years of damp and draught, crude repairs, constant complaints and occasional 'bodgings' by workmen told to spend as little as possible. An appeal to the local public health housing inspector might achieve some marginal improvement, but he too accepted that only minimum standards of weathertightness could be applied when clearance-area action was anticipated. An eventual takeover by the housing department might still mean no improvement and only minimal action despite it being a matter of months (or even years) before a move to a decent house was possible.

On two occasions the action group organised a conducted tour of the area for a city official, along with their local councillor. On the first occasion the party explored alleyways, empty houses, chased children, caught a tatter, and listed thirty-one items requiring attention. The ageing senior public health official showed patience, resignation and shame in the discovery and organised a considerable clean-up in the next few weeks. The second occasion was intended to make a similar impression upon officials from the housing department but no one could be found from the department or from the committee to attend. The visit took place anyway, and at a public meeting a few days later officials were treated to a slide-show of what they had declined to inspect.

Again, there was a flurry of activity to secure houses better and to investigate families in particularly dire conditions. But these were but moments within a long process of dereliction and demoralisation.

The Redevelopment Process: Three Experiences

Mrs *A*, at 76 of age, had lived in her house (privately rented) since 1950, and it was taken over by the council in 1971. She came to the advice centre in 1972 and quite emphatically wanted to move as quickly as possible, for, as far as she was concerned, life in her street was intolerable. The houses opposite were being knocked down (at last) but what was worse was the vandalism to the empty property next door to her and to others in the terrace block where she lived. Her son had written to the housing department for her and she had received a reply which said that the only possibility for her to move soon would be to a flat in a multi-storey block on a far-distant estate. Now she knew perfectly well that some of her neighbours opposite had moved to the area and type of home that she wanted: a compact modern flat or maisonette in a near-by suburb. Like them she wanted to keep in touch with friends and neighbours, to carry on at her two or three social clubs in the neighbourhood just as long as her health allowed. Why, she wanted to know, was she being treated differently? It was not as if the department did not know what she wanted – she had told the man who came with the rent book in 1971 and her son had told them again in the recent letter.

The council's letter did not explain that her house was not due for demolition until 1974 and that she would get somewhere in her area of choice when that time came. It was departmental policy to give priority to immediate clearance cases, and since her chosen area and house type were extremely popular among such cases, there was no priority for her; but, as an official explained to the worker, the department wanted to seem conciliatory and so had mentioned the possibility of a distant multi-storey flat. So the only thing for Mrs *A* to do was to wait for what she wanted, and when she was told a fuller story she was more able to do so; but it made her insistence on repairs and attention to vandalism by the department more emphatic, but with limited success.

Subsequently the street in which Mrs *A* lived was put into what the housing department referred to as the 'accelerated clearance' programme. The decision was made in September 1972. No tenants were informed by the housing department, although the action group newsletter advertised the change. It made getting repairs done during the winter extremely difficult because the repairs section of the housing department seemed to believe that demolition would be immediate.

It was not until February 1973 that a housing visitor called to take Mrs *A*'s particulars and to ask where she wanted to move to. In April she and a group of neighbours were offered new flats in an immediately adjoining area. So at the last, it seemed, the department had made an effort to house a group of neighbours near to each other in a familiar neighbourhood. By then, however, Mrs *A* was in no mood to thank the department. For the last three years, since the council took over and the redevelopment had got under way, her life had been hellish.

Mr *B* had purchased his house with a council mortgage and an improvement grant in 1968. Until then he had lived with his parents and cousins in a large house near by ever since coming to Birmingham in 1965. He needed a house of his own so that his wife and children could join him from Pakistan. He did not then qualify for a council house but even had he done so would probably have chosen to buy. He took care in choosing since he reckoned that he would not be able to buy again since he was over forty and neither his mortgage prospects nor his income were likely to improve. He remembers being told by an official in the planning department that the house which he was to buy was 'safe until the twenty-first century'.

In 1970 Mr *B* approached the public health department enquiring about a further grant towards the cost of installing central heating. He was told that the house was now going to be put in a clearance area and taken over by the city council so there was no point in his installing central heating. Confirmation of this came a few months later, and in March 1972 Mr *B* became a tenant in his own house. He could see the case for clearance since so few house-owners had carried out any improvements, but he was dismayed to discover the choices open to him. He was advised that the maximum compensation likely was about £2500, which was about the amount he had spent on the house – but he knew perfectly well that this price bore no relation to the price of a comparable house since prices had been soaring since 1967. He found a house about the same size in a 'safe' street (although he now knew what that really meant!) on sale for £5000. Neither his surveyor nor the city estates department showed much interest in this yawning gap between compensation based on 'full market value' and actual market prices. He worked out that another larger mortgage for a shorter period due to his age would be very costly, certainly far in excess of his relatively low current payments. So he had to consider a council tenancy reluctantly because he valued the freedom and independence as well as the low cost of his present home. When the housing visitor called all his fears were alterted. She arrived hurriedly and unannounced when he and his wife were having lunch with their large family of young children. Before sitting down she seemed to dust off the sofa; she did not inspect the house but expressed some concern at the size of family (eight children) and was openly critical that Mr *B* allowed a relative to have a room at the house. She implied that it would not be allowed at a council house. She asked a few questions about areas of choice – anywhere near by – and left quickly. Mr *B* was extremely angry.

By this time he was a frequent caller at the advice centre and he came to ask what he should do. An enquiry telephone call to the housing department sought to establish what the visitor had recorded. It transpired that the visitor had recommended 'older property only', which meant an adverse grading due to poor housekeeping standards and no offers of any post-war property. Since the adviser knew Mr *B*'s home, and knew that few older style houses with four bedrooms existed, this was a most unjust decision. So a revisit was negotiated and the assessment changed. As a result Mr *B* was made an offer of a four-bedroomed house in another part of the middle ring. however, the quoted weekly rental was nearly £10 and he could see no way of his being able to travel to his work-place at shift hours, nor of his children staying at their present schools, so he turned it down. At the advice centre it was possible to show Mr *B* forms which showed that the *actual* rent he would have to pay would be about £5 per week. A second offer at a higher rent was for one of the houses being built in the immediate area – but he turned this down because it seemed an unmanageable design. He came to regret most bitterly these decisions (neither taken lightly nor without much family discussion), for he had to wait almost a whole year for another offer which, this time, was on a far suburban estate totally cut off from all he knew. Ironically Mr *B* had agreed to 'widen his area of choice' in the hope for an early offer but he and his family thought the distance between what he wanted and this latest offer was quite ridiculous.

In the meantime his was almost the only family left in the street and no repairs had been done to his house (despite reports and requests) for about two years. Before another offer came Mr *B* got a warning letter from the city solicitors saying that if he did not accept the next one, the council would be obliged to seek possession in the country court, and with the letter there was a form of notice to quit.

About a couple of days before the date on the notice letter he received an offer of an eminently suitable house which he was eager to accept. However, it needed some repairs and redecoration. The clerk in the lettings section told him that the house was down in her records as ready for immediate occupation and she wanted him to be a tenant from the Monday following this Thursday discussion. With some difficulty he pursuaded her that that was out of the question and that it needed attention. She agreed to investigate. He then heard nothing for several weeks and assumed that he would not get the house. His children spotted that workmen had been to the house; he visited it and found out from the foreman that a full repair and complete redecoration had been carried out. When he contacted the department he was told that this was at his request and he would be expected to take the tenancy just as soon as the workmen finished. By now his own house stood alone amidst total demolition. He moved in May 1975, two years after receiving his first offer. The experience had done nothing to alter his view of the advantages of owner-occupation and to the end he was a reluctant tenant, sceptical of the advantages his local council house brought him. What annoyed him most was the way all the officials he saw expected him to show gratitude.

Mr and Mrs *C* got exactly what they had hoped and prayed for without a struggle or a protest. Like other families, they were appalled by the change that had happened in the area. They could remember when the street lights (gas-lighted) had notices on them prohibiting spitting, dogs fouling the footpath, and littering, and when people took notice of such things, when housewives washed not just front steps but the black-tile pavements as well, and when backyards were unfenced and 'neighbouring' was common and valued. They remembered the first changes, the first house improvements, and the increasing privacy and fencing of yards and gardens and then the other changes and the demolitions and the slow and awful decline. They had not minded too much – they had moved into a good-sized and well-modernised house from a 'good' landlord and were active in clubs and groups locally, and so enjoyed the area despite everything. But what made them exceptional was that they actually feared being moved out to the near-by suburbs. They wanted to stay in a small old house in the neighbourhood. They had asked, but they did not expect – after all, they said, 'you know what Bush House housing department is like, don't you?' They did not want anyone to make any special request for them:

'you know Bush House – better leave alone'. They were relieved and amazed, in about equal proportions, when they got what they wanted. In their surprise, perhaps, is the clearest indication of the kind of relationship which prevails between those who manage redevelopment and those who experience it.

Conclusions

The Impossibility of Planning

Readers familiar with the literature about redevelopment and slum clearance may be forgiven their impatience with this same old story of delay, incompetence, insensitivity and demoralisation. There are, no doubt, literally dozens of cities and neighbourhoods where a similar sort of story could be told. Why should these problems persist? We know that several areas within Birmingham were concurrently receiving treatment little different from that reported here; and we know that a stream of local complaints arose from earlier phases of the city's comprehensive redevelopment schemes.

It is tempting to focus on the mistakes and absurdities of the planners and their succession of plans which had pretensions of comprehensiveness but which effected piecemeal dereliction and decay, or on the sickening insensitivity of housing-management staff in their relations with local residents, and to rehearse recommendations for better planning, improved management, effective communication and basic co-ordination among the various officials and departments concerned. Yet all such reasonable proposals have been made previously and will no doubt be made again. Birmingham is a large, relatively wealthy city with a record and a claim to employ competent officials and to have had coherent management and leadership.

We have stressed earlier the scale of Birmingham's post-war redevelopment enterprise and would not gainsay that impressive record. But we are more concerned to explore the meaning of that achievement for those affected: for the ordinary citizens of Birmingham in whose name and for whose benefit it was all done. What we would question is the nature of the control that was executed by the city council over the process. Our story about this small part of a redevelopment area reveals a considerable amount about that control and provides a necessary context for any discussion of the quality of management and planning and how they might be changed for the better.

We would suggest that our story at times shows the *impossibility* of planning. When in 1955 huge areas of Birmingham's inner city were bravely designated for comprehensive redevelopment by 1975, those taking the decision were setting in motion processes which meant that, ultimately, ownership of the land would be transferred to the city council. Planners' blight has a vicious circular effect whereby it worsens the physical situation to a state where redevelopment is the only possible outcome; but until the actual date of council takeover and demolition the planners wreak the havoc they subsequently take credit for clearing up. In the intervening period, however, much is out of their control.

So, in our area in the twenty long years from its first being labelled a comprehensive development area to the final approval of the last compulsory-purchase order, the local housing market was affected, but not controlled, by the city council. The housing inspectors' attention during this time roamed through the area selecting blocks of houses for immediate clearance, reprieving others and benignly neglecting others.

However, the rate of acquisition was out of their control as the housing department calculated, guessed or hoped for a high rate of new house-building that would make continuing clearance possible – but the rate of building was only partially under the control of the housing department, which also had to respond to other demands for council housing arising from other parts of the market. Until the late 1960s Birmingham was successful in maintaining a large building programme and a high rate of clearance. However, from about 1970, when finally it had acquired substantial land in our study area, the council had insufficient control over the building industry and was further hampered by central-government restrictions inimicable to a high rate of new council-house-building. So there was delay and further dereliction, despite 'plans' to the contrary. It was not simply a case of lack of co-ordination between the various departments involved with different stages in the twenty years of planning which caused blight and its attendant discomforts and chaos; rather, none of the departments possessed control over the processes involved so as to be able to plan in detail for the people concerned. That is what we mean by the 'impossibility of planning'.

Questions of Power: Housing Class and Urban Managers

The case study suggests then that in the management of redevelopment the capacity of the local authority to maintain a high building rate was of fundamental importance. In our concluding chapter we will have to examine that power in greater detail.

What kind of power was possessed by the local people? What analogies to a market situation are discernable here? What kinds of participation in the process appeared possible? On the surface what possible reasons are there for a clash of interests between the managers and the managed, given the nature of local demands ('wishes' is perhaps a more apt word)?

A swift, assured, competently time-tabled redevelopment programme would have satisfied most residents; they could know where they stood and be able to believe in the plans, promises and proposals (such as they were) that were offered. Very few of the residents were opposed to redevelopment. Most people looked forward to the prospect of a better, modern house in a different area. Some looked on that as of right not simply because they were losing their own home and deserved something in exchange but because of the expectations of standards and values in housing to which they had become accustomed. It was consistent with these expectations to find intolerable the filth and dereliction which accompanied the redevelopment.

As in the previous case study we should note that few residents in our area had the resources to escape; no doubt in the earlier stages there were those who sold their houses to the council and purchased what they could with the proceeds. But for the majority that kind of market power had been withdrawn as total local-authority control spread over the area. Furthermore, despite the apparently similar conditions, the administrative complexity placed individuals and groups in a very different practical relationship: owners and tenants of houses were treated differently and had varieties of access to alternatives. So the notion of 'housing class' – common relationship to the means of housing – is singularly unhelpful in this situation.

But given this diversity of access and relative uniformity of interest in swift sensitive redevelopment, what is one to make of the style of management effected and the nature of the relationship achieved between managers and managed? To consider it as an effective management system may be instructive and bring out the differences in interests between the managers and the managed. Perhaps those appalling conditions are the clue to what is effective. The interests of management are to parry protest and induce patience, since managerial control over the process is partial. Discretionary rehousing removes in time those who might protest too much; a dependent clientele for the gradual working out of the redevelopment process is made and sustained – and after years of horror, people are pleased to accept what is offered them by way of alternative housing accommodation and few unrealistic demands are made by redevelopment families upon the housing department. Thus from the point of view of many in the city council it works.

There are some significant side-effects of this system, or style, of management. The nature of the controls over the process are never questioned. The council presents an *illusion* of official competence which is never scrutinised since the terms in which complaints and protests are discussed are in the terms of that competence. Whenever councillors, officials or independent advisers meet individuals, it is to explore and examine what can be done for that individual within the terms of some departmental brief or set of guidelines. It is difficult for that individual to see who is controlling what. Even to councillors the system is extraordinarily opaque. And usually *something* can be done: a visit can be arranged, a repair put in hand, a family moved, so to all concerned it is not an inflexible system but one in which the basis for decisions and the scope for change is real but unpredictable.

The extent and variety of constraints influencing redevelopment are also rarely made visible or explained. In our study area the delay over the new house-building was forcefully explained as reflecting government controls over local authorities. But this was in the context of a very limited lobby for local rehousing, and occurred at the end of the delay period, not during it, so it was more an explanation in justification and support of the system than anything else. The broader issues of housing need and city-wide policies were never provided except to reduce the effectiveness of local protest and to establish the greater knowledge and competence of officials as against local spokesmen. The individualised treatment of issues, of course, did not provide opportunities for elaborate explanations and there were few other times and places where such explanations could be given. Indeed, such explanations which indicate limits on the control and competence of officials would have sounded strange in a context where officials and councillors tended to stress their control and competence.

The management style was effective in making residents feel

dependent upon the services of the managers; at each and every turn their powerlessness was underlined. The idea that the process was being managed in their interests, for their benefit, by their political representatives, with their money, was beyond belief. This is a theme which will be examined further but the essential effect we would make for this story about redevelopment is how the effect of management was to depoliticise utterly the context and the process and to reinforce the sense of powerlessness in local people.

Chapter 5
Case Study 3: Saving for Improvement

Introduction

Our third case study is concerned with the redevelopment process, the introduction of house and area improvement policies, and with allocation policies regarding the use of older homes by the local housing department. The scale is smaller here; we are concerned with the fate of a small block of some 100 houses which were once within the boundaries of an area for comprehensive redevelopment so designated, like that in the previous chapter, in 1955.

However, nationally and locally from the mid-1960s, the drift of policy was in search of alternatives to the seeming inevitability of the decay–blight–demolish–rebuild cycle. The 1969 Housing Act provided a new basis for grant-aided improvement of older houses and, following the Act, a government circular instructed local authorities to 'consider urgently all possible steps to promote house improvements in their area' (Ministry of Housing and Local Government 79/70). One way of doing this could be the retention of houses previously scheduled for clearance.

This chapter concerns one such group of houses snatched from the path of the bulldozers and 'saved for improvement'. The block in question consists of about 100 houses on two sides of a triangular wedge of land; the base of the triangle, with old houses affected by a 'future road-widening line' was, however, not saved. All the houses open directly on to the street and most have no hallways. They were built with two rooms and a scullery downstairs, an outside toilet in a small yard and a small garden beyond and three bedrooms upstairs. In some of the houses a bathroom and toilet have been installed in the smallest upstairs room; in others, part of the downstairs area has been adapted and extended to provide a kitchen, bathroom and toilet. The majority of houses, however, were unimproved in 1970, when the city reviewed houses in its clearance areas in order to determine whether any could be retained.

When the review occurred the housing department owned some twenty-five of the houses, a further twenty-five were privately rented (mostly unfurnished) with the other fifty in owner-occupation. Many of the owners were Asians who were relative newcomers to the city and the area. The council tenants were of more recent arrival and tended to be families of mixed sizes and of various ethnic backgrounds. A group of long-established English households was to be found in all three tenure types.

The comprehensive development area (C. D. A.), in which these houses had been since 1955, was large, the individual clearance areas numerous and progress was slow. Even though there was some new building on adjacent land during the 1960s, it tended to be lost and invisible beside a vast wasteland of derelict houses, decaying industrial premises, patched old housing, cleared and partially cleared sites and the occasional row of shops. Only in 1970 was a *planning* compulsory-purchase order prepared to permit the acquisition of fit housing, shops and industrial premises to permit large-scale redevelopment. The 'saving' of the hundred houses in our street block needs to be seen in relation to that fifteen-year 'programme' of redevelopment.

An important feature of the process of redevelopment was the willingness of the city council to purchase owner-occupied property by agreement in advance of any compulsory-purchase order. This occurred on quite a considerable scale throughout comprehensive development areas and explains why the council owned twenty-five properties in the retained block in this area. Acquired property was, and still is, used by the housing department as part of its over-all stock. Some of it was in relatively good condition and, at the time of acquisition, was expected to have a long life and was treated accordingly both by the housing department and tenants, many of whom would have chosen to live there. However, as time passes and the projected life of acquired property shortens, the housing department's repair and allocation policies alter. As little as possible is done in the way of repairs and the properties become deemed suitable only for tenants graded as 'poor' by virtue of 'housekeeping standards' and rent-paying propensity – the choice element declines and the sort of tenants rapidly become those who have little choice of being offered anywhere else.

The combination of the long, slow process of piecemeal demolition, scant regard for repairs, and lettings to a particular kind of tenant, some of whom have been moved from another redevelopment area now being cleared, contribute to the dreadful living conditions which frequently characterise life in one of Birmingham's comprehensive development areas.

This background had important considerations for the residents of the 'saved' street block and for an organised attempt, involving a local neighbourhood association and a community worker, to involve people in the process of improvement.

The Community Association

Within the C. D. A. in the early 1960s the effects of large-scale immigration, racial hostility and the emergence of a major problem of prostitution and soliciting in a small group of streets led a number of local people, priests, vicars and welfare workers to start a local association to provide supporting projects, a pressure group and a focus of family care and concern for the neighbourhood. Initially it was housed in the 'vice area', but when that was cleared its headquarters moved to a new community centre in the heart of the cleared, but as yet unbuilt, section of the C. D. A. From that base it continued to be involved in dealing with some of the side-effects of the redevelopment process, seeking to make explicit criticisms of the destructive effect of redevelopment policies and to explore alternatives. In 1970 its attention turned to the neighbourhood beyond the boundary of the C. D. A. and started to stress the need for clear and definite planning statements about that neighbourhood in order to prevent the blight and decay of redevelopment spreading further. The argument was one for sensible improvement policies to replace large-scale clearance.

In 1971 the association took two steps to advance this kind of action.

It organised a housing exhibition to test out local feeling and opinion about the future of the neighbourhood and it raised funds for, and appointed, a new community worker to promote this work in an area threatened by redevelopment. The work had some fairly well-defined aims: to change the council's attitude to slum clearance; to stimulate the emergence of residential groups and allow a dialogue between residents and the council on prospects for the neighbourhood; also, to increase the flow of information to local people with particular emphasis on stimulating the take-up of improvement grants. The person appointed to the job was a relatively inexperienced community worker who had just finished a college course. As part of his course he had spent some time on a placement with the association and had organised the housing exhibition.

It was at the exhibition in April 1971 that the association members and the community worker learned of the change in designation of the street block from being part of the C. D. A. scheduled for acquisition and clearance, to being an area which was 'to be retained'. A map provided by the council showing the future lay out of the new development indicated the change. Thus when the new project started in October 1971, it was on the new worker's agenda to explore the nature and implications of this change and to find ways in which local people might become involved in this planned change for their streets.

During the pilot stage of our research, one of the research team had become involved with the association, the exhibition and the new project and saw that an opportunity existed for the researcher to contribute to the developing project and to learn from its attempt to relate local people to possible changes in housing and planning issues affecting the neighbourhood. As time went by, and as the new work developed, a research-action interest specifically in the fate and future of the 'saved' houses developed. A new member of the research team with interests in planning and housing worked with the community worker as a housing and planning adviser and went out to meet local residents to discuss house- and area-improvement plans. He later bought one of the houses in the area and so became directly involved as a resident in the process under study. This case study is an account of his growing awareness of the complexity of something which on the surface looked rather simple.

A Simple Case of Home Improvement?

What on the surface could be simpler? Here was a group of shabby but sound houses near a park and shops and soon to be within a new residential area. There was evidence of reasonably brisk trade in the houses and most were in owner-occupation, with a substantial number owned by the city council. Existing legislation provided generous grants to assist owners to improve and the council had now decided they were improvable after all. A local association was well placed to ensure maximum conmunication about the policy change and the scope of grant aid for improvement. Surely it would be safe to expect a fairly rapid take-up of grants and, given all the publicity relating to participation in planning, it should prove relatively easy to negotiate a scheme of environmental improvements acceptable to owners, tenants and the council. Within a few years, surely, a noticeable difference in the housing conditions would be visible for all to see and for which local residents, the association and the city council would be able to take some credit.

Five years after the changed designation, however, there was very little change visible to the eye: only a few houses had been modernised, the sites near by were still awaiting clearance, the timing of any change at the base of the triangle was still uncertain, the streets had still not been declared a General Improvement Area and there were no signs of environmental improvement. To explain this we need to explore further the assumptions and practices of those who manage the process of improvement; of those who, in this instance, sought to mediate between the managers and the managed; and, crucially, we need to look at the residents and how they viewed and reacted to the proposals.

The Local Authority Involvement

We have already mentioned that the C. D. A. in which the street blocks were located was large and the work of redevelopment had been in process since the early 1960s. Undoubtedly a major factor in delay in the latter years had been the sharp decline in the rate of council-house-building after 1968. However, it would seem to be the case that the programming of the final planning compulsory-purhcase order and the time such orders take to complete added to the over-all delay in the redevelopment of the area. It certainly reduced the number of large sites available for housing starts because of the scattered diversity of shops, factories and industrial premises in the area. The delay of compulsory purchase until 1970 ensured, therefore, that there were, fifteen years after the declaration of the comprehensive development areas, still blocks of houses standing whose future could be reviewed.

The mechanics of the review were fairly simple. Officers in the planning and redevelopment section of the public works department liaised with the local public health inspectors in considering possible blocks for retention. No detailed examination was made of either structure or ownership, just a cursory look at exteriors and a reliance on the records kept by the health inspectors. Our particular block was a good candidate because it was on the fringe of the C. D. A. and would not affect plans already prepared for redevelopment in the rest of the area.

The council's planning sub-committee considered the recommendation which was then passed by the main committee and ratified by the council. It became clear subsequently that it was simply a decision not to demolish – no further policy proposals were made for two years and no indication was given by the planners about life expectation or grant eligibility of the houses because such decisions rested with another department – the public health department. Residents and owners were not informed of any change.

It emerged subsequently, in private discussions between the community worker and a local public health inspector, that the decision was not irreversible. Indeed, following a public meeting it became a task for the community worker to establish whether there was strong feeling against the decision and, if so, whether it could be reviewed. Until the end of 1972 there was some uncertainty about the level of grant aid available for these houses because of the uncertain assessment by the public health inspectors of the number of years life left during which the houses could be satisfactorily used. This 'lifing' of properties by the inspectors is a central and routine part of their practice. If houses were assessed as having less than a thirty-year life then they could not qualify for full grant aid. Lifing assessments of five, seven, ten and fifteen years appeared to be part and parcel of the inspectors' expertise at this time. In January 1973, however, the council published their new urban renewal policy in which the street block was linked to a larger, adjacent area of housing as part of a proposed General Improvement Area to be declared in 1975. If that proposal secured the houses finally and made full grants available, it was still uncertain in 1975 whether the houses would be included in a General Improvement Area or dealt with in some other way. Residents and owners have still not been officially told about the changes, although as a result of the work of the community association most of them have been kept informed.

The review and change in designation occurred in early 1971. Decisions about lifting were made in 1973 as part of the new policy. Only since then has it been possible for owners to obtain improvement grants and prospective owners to obtain city council mortgages. The council would no longer buy 'ahead of clearance' and would improve the houses it owned in the streets and, in 1974, one such house was opened amidst considerable publicity as a show house to demonstrate the improvement potential. The timing of environmental improvements, clearance and rebuilding in parts of the adjacent C. D. A., however, were still shrouded in mystery.

The Community Association and its Worker

The association, founded in 1961 by workers in the neighbourhood, despite some hopes, claims and a low membership fee, never succeeded in becoming an organisation of local people. It remained a loose federation of those professionally involved in the area – schoolteachers, priests, social workers and probation officers, together with a small number of local people usually with some specific interest or activity. The association sponsored or provided a charitable base for a number of local projects, for example playgroups, an adventure playground and advisory services. The new community worker was expected to administer these existing projects as well as develop the new work of finding alternatives to clearance and of involving local residents.

The collective experience of those involved in the association and of the worker was that the main problem of the neighbourhood was the destruction to morale caused by the redevelopment programme and fears that, without positive action, the council might easily extend the scope of redevelopment even further. Although the aims of the project were fairly clear, how they might be achieved was never really specified. The community worker was not an expert conversant with the technicalities of public health, housing, planning law and lore, nor about improvements, architecture or building. He was a community worker and his main skill was seen to be an ability to meet people, discuss and explain things with them, to have some ideas for getting local residents' associations going, and to be able to liaise with relevant officials and experts to get them to discuss and explain how residents' interests could be translated into action. He was seen essentially as a 'go-between'; it was assumed – perhaps 'hoped' is a more appropriate term – that residents were interested in 'having a say' in the future of the neighbourhood and in some kind of collective action and liaison with the city council. It was not assumed that the council would simply accede to well-organised residents' requests; rather, it was expected that a process of negotiation would be necessary. At the outset it was assumed that if there were any preconceived future for the neighbourhood, it was more likely to be in terms of eventual demolition and it would be very hard to convince the council that improvement was viable. The belief that improvement was obviously 'better than clearance' found the association's committee, the worker and the research team in full accord, although none had worked out in detail the answer to the question: better for whom?

The council's decision to retain some houses in the C. D. A. sounded a very good idea, the first sign perhaps of a change of heart. The community worker assumed at first that the decision, once taken, was final and the task to be undertaken was to let people know the good news, involve them in finding out what could be done and to *organise* contact between officials and local residents to get things happening.

Although employed specifically on a new project in the 'threatened' neighbourhood, the worker found many distractions in the old area and on existing projects to prevent him actually starting on the new work until the summer of 1972. His work base continued at an office in the recently built community centre within the C. D. A.

During the summer of 1972 he had some discussions with local public health inspectors who indicated that the decision to retain the street block was not completely closed. Although the houses had not been included in the final planning compulsory-purchase order, future clearance action was not ruled out – it depended upon the residents and what improvements they brought about. It also became clear that there was some uncertainty about the lifing of the houses which would influence the sort and level of grant aid available. These discussions firmly convinced the worker that his task must get under way to marshall local residents' action to resolve the uncertainty.

He started to visit the homes to explain the change of plan and the possibilities that this gave, and to find out who lived there and their attitudes towards the proposals. Stressing the value of a residents' association for the street, he had sent a letter to all residents telling them briefly what had happened and said he would be calling on

them to discuss matters. But progress was very slow, and he enlisted
some help from students in making the necessary contacts. Once the
visiting had been done he called a meeting in a near-by hall in July 1972
at which a residents' association organised a public meeting for all
residents in October at which a local public health inspector would
explain the current situation.

The community worker found no great enthusiasm for the proposals;
at the best there was scepticism, but also a lot of apathy and some
outright hostility. We will examine these in greater detail in the
following sections, but here it is sufficient to note that this unexpected
lack of eagerness to 'participate' was both disappointing and confusing
to the worker. When these diverse feelings surfaced at the public
meeting, moreover, the health inspector added to the worker's
difficulties by claiming that the community association's pressure
caused the change from demolition to retention, and by adding that if
the people did not want the houses saved then the decision could be
reversed. All that could be made clear was that the council now
reckoned on a fifteen-year life for the houses and this *should* mean the
maximum rate of improvement grants.

This meeting left the residents' association something of a paper tiger,
incapable of progress until its internal conflict of opinion was resolved.
It left the community worker and the community association in a
quandary, for, committed to improvement *and* to an idea of local
residents' self-determination, what happened when these ideals came
into conflict? The worker was also uneasy about continuing work with
the residents' association and, as there was plenty of other things to be
done, he did very little with it.

He was not completely inactive in the streets, however, since the
meeting had left a clear need for a thorough examination of residents'
wishes and an explanation of the potentiality for area, as well as house,
improvements and the possibility of a General Improvement Area
declaration for the street block. It was like going back to square one.

So a second bout of 'finding out' saw the involvement of a member of
the research team and the emergence of what we call 'research–action'.
As it got underway, however, it became clear to the worker and the
researcher/adviser that the city council's own thinking was undergoing
a considerable change and this culminated in the urban renewal policy
which eliminated the category of fifteen-year lifing for houses and
included all houses either in General Improvement Areas with long life
and grant aid for environmental and home improvement, or 'renewal

areas' where some houses would be cleared and some retained and improved. Our block was included within a proposed General Improvement Area. This meant that there was no longer anything for the community association, the residents' association and the community worker to fight for since the doubts were now resolved, although there now remained problems of progress, implementation and timing.

The community worker was by this time based at a shop-front advice centre in the immediate vicinity, and with the adviser he tackled individual problems, and began to explore, with a housing association and a group of architectural students, a way of involving residents. That work, as we shall see, proved as problematical as the first phases of participation.

The Residents' Association

About forty people came to the first meeting called by the worker in July 1972 – mostly, one would guess, to find out what was being said rather than to take part in any long-term action. At that meeting and after much persuasion and insistence by the worker, about fourteen people somewhat reluctantly agreed to form a committee and to meet a week or two later. The worker managed to persuade two of the people to be chairman and secretary, but from the start it was clear that the role of the worker would be crucial if the idea of a residents' association was to take hold and mean anything to those involved.

Committee meetings were few, unstructured and, for the worker, uncomfortable, since he found himself being both secretary and chairman, and more directive than he had supposed. Moreover, there was still no unanimity about the value of the change from demolition to retention. Those most keen for the change tended to be the Asians, one or two of whom came to meetings, but who rarely spoke. The most outspoken committee members stressed the problems of the wider area, of prostitutes, 'problem families', the attitude of the housing department and the 'takeover' of the road by 'immigrants'. Some on the committee, it became clear, resented the change because it seemingly withdrew their only opportunity of a move, sooner rather than later, to a decent council house in a decent area. Bickering at committee meetings prevented the emergence of any collective feeling, and when it came to the public meetings with the public health department the inexperience of the leadership, the dependency on the worker and the rifts of opinion were all too apparent.

Thereafter the association took on an entirely nominal existence. It was never a real association of local residents, although the worker remained in touch with residents and kept alive some notion of its viability. When in August 1973 the direction of the community workers's interest and that of the adviser changed in the light of the council's new policy, the association was revived and a meeting was arranged to discuss the worker's and adviser's ideas about improvement and to gain the formal support of the association.

Those who came to the association tended to be people with strong feelings, often a grievance, hoping that through the meeting they may be able to lodge their complaint more forcibly. Others were people who wanted to stay and hoped that things would improve but looked for a lead and direction from the worker or the adviser as people who knew about such things. But as soon as the community association's advice centre got under way, then for many there was less need for their association since you could always count on help from that quarter.

Apathy and disinterest are wrong definitions of this local feeling and disinclination to get together in a collective effort to change things. First, it was made very clear at all the meetings that there *were* very strong feelings and people willing and able to express themselves. But what was seen as the targets of this strong feeling were some families and some aspects of council policy (particularly on housing) and the suggested lines of action were along other directions. Second, it was quite true that the technical aspects of home and area improvement needed explication from an expert who could be trusted – so to defer to the worker and adviser was, at this level, extremely sensible. But, most important of all, there were genuinely discordant interests within the street block, different bases for action, different hopes, feelings and opportunities which it would be naïve to suppose could find expression through the form of a residents' association. And, anyway, that idea, its form and procedures were all unfamiliar elements offered and imposed by outsiders and did not arise from or reflect the common experience of the local people.

Residents

Our understanding of the local view of the proceedings started as the adviser got to know more people and spent more time with them. This developing contact enabled him to investigate some of the assumptions held by the community worker and himself. The assumption that by this time (summer–autumn 1973) most people would be aware of the official change in policy had to be put aside. The adviser's set of alternative possible environmental improvements (for example, providing some rear access to common garaging, or individual gardens) were met so often with blank puzzlement at first, and only after lengthy discussion was it established that some major changes to the immediate environs of the houses were feasible.

It did become clear that the decision to change the designation from clearance to retention had already had an impact; above a third of the houses were occupied by families who had moved in since 1971. Some had sold up and gone; some had died and the houses sold by the landlords; there was some turnover in the council houses and a housing association had bought both tenanted and vacant houses from a private landlord, and its tenants were newcomers.

So the resident population was in no way homogeneous, stable or 'trapped' – rather, it was characterised by diversity, mobility and, indeed, instability. Many residents did know about improvement grants and some were keen to make a start, but the process was mysterious, cloaked with uncertainty and hardly anyone had actually done anything about starting work. Many were waiting to see what would happen to the council houses, and tenants, of course, were not clear whether landlords would or could be forced to do the work.

There had been a steady succession of new Asian households to the streets, most moving from another part of the neighbourhood either through demolition or the formation of a new household. Frequently paying cash or buying on a bank loan, the small terrace houses were relatively cheap and convenient for work and community facilities. Attracted by the opportunity of a house to buy rather than rent, many of these families had either not been aware of the clearance proposals, or had seen the house as a relatively short-term measure, hoping to buy again as and when necessary. Many were not particularly interested in the area as such and were rarely concerned with environmental improvements but almost invariably had no wish to leave except, perhaps, for a bigger house near by, if the family outgrew its present accommodation. Often quite keen to make improvements to their houses, many were still paying for them at quite high interest rates, which combined with relatively low incomes and large families to support did not leave much spare cash – the idea of improving the house all in one go was not appealing, at least until their mortgage was paid off.

One family, a young married couple with one child, moved in a year after the area was to be retained; the father paid a £500 deposit and raised a bank loan for £1500 which he was paying off over seven years. The house was unimproved with no bathroom and an outside toilet and was in need of repair. He had done a lot of minor items himself but got tradesmen in for jobs that he could not manage. He anticipated eagerly the rebuilding of the adjacent cleared land and the improvement of his house. But he could not afford to go ahead. The process of obtaining an improvement grant and a builder would be bad enough, but because of his existing outgoings he would be ineligible for a city council loan towards his share of the improvement costs.

Another couple of Asian households that benefited from the change in plans have now left. The first consisted of three cousins and one of their wives who bought a terraced house outright for £450 in 1969. All were working at a local bakery, doing large amounts of overtime and sending money home to Bangladesh. They never saw England as home. Informed of the change in plans, aware of the implications of this for the value of their house and keen to return to their homeland they were able to sell for £2000 and leave so much the richer. Another Asian family has also left. They bought their house in 1966 on a bank loan, not knowing its future. Hearing of the clearance proposals they decided to wait until demolition and hope for adequate compensation. The change of plan enabled them to go; the family had outgrown the house anyway and they could now sell. But they did not go far – only to a bigger house a few hundred yards away.

Of many other Asians, newcomers and established, the adviser found out relatively less. Language difficulties, even with the aid of an interpreter, were not easily overcome. But from those conversations that were more successful, and after discussions with an interpreter who was another local community worker, a picture began to emerge. Above all, the house – the home – was important. In the neighbourhood generally, and in these streets in particular, houses can be *bought* quite cheaply, and now in these streets there is no longer any danger of clearance. There was correspondingly little appreciation that the city would actually require certain kinds of improvements to individual houses. The old policies – seen as threats – of clearance, inadequate compensation, and a choice between a rented council house or flat or moving to another bought property were understood – they knew that their houses would be taken from them. So often this was difficult to understand as there seemed no sense in pulling down houses that they found satisfactory. If the houses were not to be pulled down, then was that not the end of the matter? Would they not be left alone now?

More than that the notion of people getting together to work with the council and prepare plans to improve 'the environment' was often culturally incomprehensible. Why should people mess around with back access? Anyway, most had little intention of spending their own money on such things. Obviously there were variations. The men, who were more integrated into the host society, understood more about what was happening than did the women. There were differences of origin, of religion, of temperament, attitude and income; but for present purpose these differences were less relevant than the common factor of being different. Brought together by what they had in common, a cultural and class position, they were not likely to get together on housing issues without a common threat, and even then only with difficulty. The house, as objective existence and symbol of economic strength and independence, was critical. Until, or unless, there was a specific power relationship *demanding* some action, then things were fine as they were.

We referred to the arrival of Asians as a continuation of a pattern going on for several years. In 1973 they were the largest group of newcomers but by no means a majority of the streets' population. Many of the houses were still owned or tenanted by ageing English families who had been in the streets for years; and for those families it was frequently the number and type of newcomers who were held responsible for the 'decline' of their area.

We found that *length of residence* was a far more important link to attitudes and feelings than was tenure. Some of the old owners had been tenants who bought cheaply after the Second World War. These houses had for many years been coming on to the market as owners moved or when tenants died and landlords realised their capital. For some of these older residents there was a feeling of having been trapped in an area that had undergone real change. They now wished they had done what their neighbours of old did – sell up while they could – or while the council were still buying 'ahead of clearance'. The older owners found themselves too old to tackle another mortgage and the houses could not be sold at a price which would enable them to buy something better elsewhere. Owners were not eligible to go on the housing waiting list and the elderly tenants who were registered were considered 'adequately housed' as far as the housing department was concerned and had a very low priority.

Frequently there were family tensions. The streets had acquired a justifiable reputation for vice, with prostitutes awaiting customers on a near-by street corner and 'kerb-crawlers' on the prowl. Combined with the general dereliction of the clearance area and poor street lighting, it can be a somewhat desolate place, particularly for the mother or her daughter returning home on a dark evening. The man works locally. He has a group of friends that is spatially more scattered but collects at the local pubs; he is not so immediately affected or annoyed as his wife by the whores and attendant cars. Many of these working-class women do not go out to work; they have to put up with annoyances that their men can shrug off or overlook.

This group was most frequently resentful about change – the whores, the wave of immigrants, the 'problem families', dirt, decay and demolition. Some had previously tried to get grants to improve their houses, but could not do so because of the clearance proposals. Now a lot of them are too old to bother and not sure if it is worth it anyway.

One such family has lived in a house they bought as sitting tenants for forty years; they are now retired. They have been through the whole saga of planning uncertainty and it has caught them just wrong – when they had finished paying for the house and had the spare cash to improve they could not get a grant. They got used to the fact of clearance, hoped for some compensation and dreamed of being rehoused in a bungalow in the suburbs. The old lady did not realise that they would probably be offered a flat and she was horrified when the adviser pointed this out! She did not *want* to stay in the neighbourhood: 'It wasn't so bad when I was working, but now I just go round friends and relations' houses; I can't stand being at home during the daytime.' She feared that the council would make them do expensive improvements that they could not afford and that they would have to sell to the council, pay rent and still not be able to get out. She and her husband had hoped for somewhere better for their retirement than here, which she referred to as 'a building site'; for her, the prostitutes, the 'problem families' and the disruption of clearance have become intolerable. Improvement to the area – to *her* house? 'It's too late.' She remembered the war, when, in spite of the hardships' we were all happy, but now, I don't think it's worth bothering. . . . I've never been so depressed as I am now.'

Most of the others in a similar position, though, 'put up with it', while even she fluctuated in her mood; many others were happy enough to make the best of things, look forward to the possibility of seeing the area 'get better'. They did not want to leave the neighbourhood and hoped that 'they' (the council) would 'do something' to see that improvement took place. Often voicing the same sort of feelings about prostitutes and 'problem families' whom they usually believed to be to blame for 'bringing the area down', more so even than 'the immigrants', there was a 'live and let live' tolerance and acceptance of change.

But for the fact of tenure, the older tenants were indistinguishable from their owner-occupier counterparts. One of those, the secretary of the residents' association, came to England over twenty years ago, leaving his wife in Dublin while he looked for work. His first stopping-place was in a neary-by road where he got lodgings. He got on well enough with the landlord, but wanting to bring his wife over he needed somewhere bigger. He had the idea of renting a big house and taking in lodgers at a small profit. The idea was a disaster, only one man paying his rent regularly, so he got rid of all the other tenants. However, this meant that the rent he was paying was beyond his means, especially as he had two children. His wife registered with the housing department and 'out of the blue' they were offered their present place. It was their first offer; the street being 'very different then', they were delighted. He was already (and still is) a regular in the local pub and they were given no indication that the house would eventually be coming down. He did not want to move, his roots in Birmingham were all in the neighbourhood, he seemed to know just about everyone in the local Irish community. Almost infinitely tolerant, mischievous and peaceful, he was tremendously fond of his children – the son a computer operator and the daughter doing well at grammar school.

He had vague plans to go back to Ireland. He never wanted to buy a house and he would wait at least until his daughter left school. Meanwhile his house was in good condition. He did many repairs himself as he could not be bothered to wait for the council, but did not really care if the house was 'improved' or not. It had a bathroom and was in fair condition; they were happy enough as they were. His wife had plenty of friends locally and she was a very cheerful, easy-going woman. They would probably not get a transfer easily, but they did not want one; things could be a lot better, they were 'all right' as they were.

He had got views on the 'problem families' – more tolerant than anyone else in the streets – and on anything else you liked to raise. But he could be serious – a working-class philosopher of sorts. He was

persuaded to be secretary of the residents' association, which he agreed
to do seriously but reluctantly, believing that 'it's up to you' (i.e. the
community worker and the adviser).

Other council tenants, who often wanted to be rehoused in the
neighbourhood, came to the streets as a result of clearance elsewhere.
Some eight or nine years ago the streets were seen by them as a good
solution to their problem. In only one or two cases were they ever
told that these streets were then marked down for clearance. This was
the 'better part' of the area, away from that part of the clearance area
that was notorious for 'vice'. Mainly white, these council tenants
shared many feelings with the older owner-occupiers. The streets have
'gone down', some just want to leave, others are more philosophical and
rarely complain.

This group tend to remember 'how nice an area it was . . . but it is
different now'. Among these was a woman separated from her husband
and caring for two young teenage children who was moved from an
early demolition section of the comprehensive development area eight
years ago. She was full of complaints and acrimony, feeling that the
council had been letting the street run down. She tried to get repairs
done, but nothing happened: 'You try to keep the place clean but you
get no help at all.' Respectable, working-class, Irish, she hated the area
and most of all the people in it: 'Unless the people change, then God
help us!' She can 'put a finger on' the bad ones. Of one woman, it is 'well
known she is a prostitute and does business in someone's house in the
next street'. She blamed 'problem families' for her problems and the
council for putting them in the area; insecure and frightened, she
wanted to go as she was 'ashamed of the place', with no interest in seeing
the area improved.

Her life was 'absolute torture'. When some Midlands Electricity
Board workmen left displaced paving stones in the street, causing an
accident, nothing was done: 'It wouldn't happen elsewhere . . . they
don't care.' 'They' are the council, the police 'anybody like that'. A
friend who works in Bush House told her that the council 'couldn't care
less' about the neighbourhood, and, '*that's proof*, isn't it?'

She applied for a transfer in August 1972 and she was still waiting
three years later. She wanted a flat or maisonette in the rebuilt part of
the adjacent redevelopment; with relatives near by, children settled at
local schools, she would feel 'more secure' there. She has probably got
her transfer by now as her 'housekeeping standards' are good, but it
would have come more quickly if she 'widened her area of choice'. But

she did not want to go far; she might have decided to stay put if and when something happened to make the immediate area more to her liking: 'Every family that moves in gets worse and worse . . . there's no decent people any more.' But she *did* get on with some neighbours – her complaints to the adviser were perhaps melodramatic rather than sincere. She had real fears, at times, but many were of her own invention. The general degeneration of the house, of physical conditions in the area, coupled with her personal hopelessness, made her both a sad person and yet almost a comic in her prejudice and narrowmindedness.

But not all council tenants were dissatisfied and wanted to move away. One family lived in grossly overcrowded conditions in a council house. The household consists of the man, his wife, two sons and daughter, plus his brother, his wife and their son and daughter. Originally from Pakistan, he was in England from 1957 to 1963 and then came back to England seven years ago, with his wife and eldest son, and moved in with relatives four streets away. Soon after, with the aid of a bank loan, he and his brother bought a cheap, short leased house in another local street. This was taken over by the council when that part of the road was acquiried for clearance. Wanting to stay in the neighbourhood and to be rehoused together, they accepted their first offer, which was the house in which they were living. When they first moved in there were only three children between the two sets of parents. The offer came quickly, after two or three weeks, and they were happy enough with their house despite being rather overcrowded and suffering all sorts of delays in getting essential repairs done.

They did not have, or were not willing to discuss, any complaints about the area. Again it was 'all right'. Although they would have liked a bigger house, they did not want to move far away to get it. The adviser was involved over an eight-month period during which time some essential repairs were done, albeit slowly; and yet, they maintained, they liked living in the street and in the neighbourhood. It was better than their previous houses, and, generally, the area presented no problems for them. The so-called local 'problems' so often mentioned by English, Irish and West Indian residents meant nothing to them. The only thing that specifically troubled them was various people walking down the back passage. They had no specific trouble from these people (who were mainly prostitutes and their clients), they just did not like the fact that the garden was split into two by alleys and thus open to anyone. Thus they were quite keen on the back-access proposals, but as tenants they had little say in what would actually happen.

As for the future, they were happy enough *where* they were; and so long as the place was not actually falling down or awash they would not complain. A few more children, of course, were on the cards and they would have to move as they grew older. Either one family would be rehoused or they would all go to a bigger place. When we knew them they were not seeking this and they were not likely to get a transfer unless they pushed for one – but, then, stranger things do happen at Bush House. So only time will tell.

It was amongst the most recent newcomers that we found the notorious 'problem families' whom the older, established residents so resented. Most of these families had already been council tenants before coming to the street block; in some cases they became tenants when the council compulsorily acquired the property they were living in, and in other cases they came after being shifted from two or three slum properties that had been cleared.

None of them wanted to move to an outer district of Birmingham, and houses of the kind to be found in these streets were fast becoming a rare commodity within the neighbourhood as other, old, council property was rapidly being demolished. A couple were prostitutes before they came, and still did a little part-time whoring, though their faces and figures no longer brought in what they once earned; children, drink and the passing years robbed them of the greater part of that source of income.

Not interested in environmental improvement, but more concerned with their own house conditions, which were often the worst in the streets, the families classified as 'problems' by their neighbours were not totally isolated, for they got on well enough with each other. For frequently unsupported women with three, four or more children, life was a round of bills, uncertainty and insecurity. On low incomes, stigmatised by their neighbours, usually they did not want to stay, but hoped for a new chance, something better, somewhere else. They were not likely to get it; those that wanted repairs done had long waits and were usually blamed (often justifiably) for causing the problem that required attention.

What was striking, in fact, was that there were so *few* 'problem families', perhaps six out of the hundred households. However, popular parlance did not necessarily always distinguish between prostitutes and other 'problems'. There was little clear distinction at all – just a general stereotyping and scapegoating.

One woman told the adviser of her past – a sheltered upbringing, respectable prostitution, then the marriage that broke up, the violence and the drinking. She knew that her neighbours disliked, resented, even despised her, so she presented a front which scorned their attitude, yet she often hoped for something more, another chance, a new life. It was difficult to talk to her, for time and again she returned to her thoughts – hazy, muddled, repetitive, a bit desperate, but, in her way, courageous. 'Fuck them. . . . I'd sell my cunt again first.' There was so little one could do to help. At times, just listening without preaching or condescension seemed to help, at others she talked and talked, ending up in tears or in anger. And yet, just once or twice, but spectacularly memorable on each occasion, she seemed another woman – polished somehow, and perhaps almost elegant. When she 'put on a face', fixed her hair, wore some decent clothes, she looked like the sort of woman that they would have called 'handsome' back in her home in Scotland.

But the desperation returned, and a dream and hope that some magical figure would arrive to transport her hence to a better world – an urban equivalent perhaps of the 'cargo cults' anthropologists have described for primitive societies. It referred to the people who were going to take her away from her present situation to a new life. Once it was her brother, who would be coming to take her back to Scotland. She would not be here 'more than another three months'; then a year later her cousin in Canada was going to pay for her to go and join the family and she worried whether her convictions for prostitution would affect this. No one that the adviser spoke to knew, and when he told her this she did not seem to care, as if he was talking about someone else whose future was of no significance. Similarly, her friend, who was evicted, told the adviser of the 'brother in Essex who was coming next week' to take her to a new house in London – so she 'didn't care' about being evicted anyway.

This woman first made herself known when she burst into the advice centre to tell the adviser that 'the bailiffs' had arrived and were evicting her, despite the fact that she was up to date with the rent. He went to her house, via the back door, to meet a group of bailiffs, an official from the county court and someone from Bush House. They wanted to know what the adviser was doing, and he wanted to know what they were doing! If anything, they found his presence to their advantage as they started to talk directly to him and use him as an intermediary to explain the situation to the woman. She kept claiming that she had paid the

rent; the officer from Bush House went out and contacted his
department from a two-way car radio and was told that there were
massive arrears and that the eviction should continue. Through the
adviser, he 'explained' to the woman that, once evicted, her family
would be put somewhere else by the council. He would give her a form
saying she was homeless, she should take it to Bush House and then the
merrygoround would start again. The original court order for eviction
had been made the year before, but had been held back on condition
she pay so much per week off the arrears. Recently she had 'held back'
rent 'because of troubles' in the area – bottles thrown over the fence,
through windows and her children had been attacked. She was told
they would be evicted so she started to 'pay it off quickly'. The week
before the eviction she 'was promised' that if she paid £5 off the arrears
she would not be evicted. She had first become a council tenant through
redevelopment. Clearly classified as suitable only for 'central-area'
property, she had moved from slum to slum, ending up in our street
when the last place was pulled down. Hopeless at managing her low
income, she never managed to pay rent regularly; yet after a period of
'dossing' with friends, she and her family were rehoused yet again, as a
homeless family, by the council, a mile or two away in another house
awaiting demolition.

It would be wrong to suggest a simple set of groupings of the area's
population and their attitudes. What needs to be stressed is the variety
and diversity. This was not a small patch of trapped families: some were
recent purchasers happy to have found an opportunity of moving into
such low-cost housing; others were dependent upon the housing
department; some have been there for years and would only move if the
council made it necessary. It was this diversity of interest and
opportunity which made attempts at collective residents' action so
unlikely and which acted as a considerable constraint upon the
implementation of any house and area improvement.

There were, however, some common recurring themes in the
residents' explanations of what was happening in their street. One was a
nostalgic theme which stressed how things had changed: invasion by a
variety of outsiders had pulled the reputation of the area down. A
minority variant of this theme was that the houses had physically
decayed and should be pulled down. A more common element in the
nostalgia was, implicitly, the question: 'could it be made better again?'
Paradoxically, this optimism was shared by many of those newcomers
whom the nostalgists resented; they liked the houses, believed in their

future and wanted to see changes happen which would improve the housing situation. Both groups shared a view about the incomprehensibility of policy but a deference and acceptance that such decisions were not their business but properly the task of some ill, or never defined group – 'the council', or 'the planners'.

Neighbourhood Associations and Housing Opportunities

This study set out to explore in some detail how housing opportunities were shaped by policy, influenced by associations and understood by local people. In many respects this small group of houses illustrates the over-all complexity of policy, the limitations to associational activity and the crucial significance of the local definitions of the housing situation on actual housing action.

Policy and Choice

Council redevelopment policy has provided the crucial setting for housing action in these streets for twenty years. Council housing-allocation policy had frequently determined both who left, by rules about transfers and applications, and who came in. As the date of redevelopment drew nearer, the category of incoming council tenant changed in a way consistent with the housing department's rules and procedures of grading by 'housekeeping standards'. Also, the exclusion of newcomers to the city from eligibility for council housing at a time of substantial immigration of workers and their families meant that they were dependent upon the market provision of low-cost housing to rent and buy. So the particular social profile of residents in the street block was largely a reflection of the working-out of local housing policies.

The shift from clearance to improvement – a central-government 'directive' implemented by public health and planning officers – merely stabilised the existing situation. In one respect, however, it changed everything, since the rehousing opportunity was withdrawn. In another respect it changed nothing as the normal market and council forces remained unchanged by the exclusion of the houses from the clearance programme.

The policy decision to include the houses in a General Improvement Area was one of very great potential significance. But, again, it was a decision which was more significant in theory rather than in practice. Essentially such policies depend upon the economic rationality of owners and landlords to enhance their capital investment by grant-aided physical alterations to the fabric of the houses and the environment. Neither the owners nor the landlords of houses in the street block could believe that it was rational to invest the money even if they had it to invest. The constraints on that investment were complex:

(1) families in low-cost, owner-occupied housing frequently purchased with high-interest, short-term loans which meant relatively high weekly payments which precluded additional borrowing for improvement;

(2) owners and landlords were very aware that policies could change and change again so were taking their cues from the council's policy towards the improvement of its own houses;

(3) elderly people used to relatively low housing standards would not change unless forced to and had no obvious interest in the capital appreciation of their property – for them even their unimproved house was a home;

(4) there had been no attempt by the city council to communicate the new opportunities which potentially existed for home improvement in a way that was credible – so the policy change remained on paper with very few signs of intelligible change existing to alter people's prior definitions of the situation.

The Influence of Neighbourhood Associations

It is now part of the assumptions of both officers and local councillors that the policy change was the result of pressure from a local association and reflected local opinion. However, it should be clear from the foregoing account that the community association had no particular role in 'saving' the street block, had only articulated a generalised concern for a more humane sort of policy than those current in redevelopment areas and was in no way an association which was in touch with and representative of local opinion.

However, since in general terms the community association was interested in working out alternatives to redevelopment, and indeed had set up a project and employed a worker to do just this, it is understandable that quite a lot of time and effort should have been spent on trying to make these ends meet. But the point to be stressed is that the series of policy decisions made by the council were not made as a result of, or were in any way related to, the association's efforts. The association and the community worker followed up and were discovering the detailed local implications of the policy changes without having any causal effects on the policy-making.

The attempt to establish the residents' association presumed both a definite set of policies and some community interest to which an association would relate. The nature of policy-making and the complexity of the local situation meant that neither a social base nor a target set of issues, *as defined collectively by residents*, existed.

This does not mean that the work done by the community worker and adviser, or that the efforts of a residents' association, were without effect or value. A considerable amount of individual counselling and advising went on; the worker and community association membership (such as it was) learned just what would need to happen if improvement was to be a viable alternative to redevelopment.

The Understanding of Residents

We have described some aspects of how local residents saw the process. Many of them had become long accustomed to the vacillations and vagaries of the (largely invisible) policy-makers and there was nothing new in the way the policy change was handled. Few could credit the community association and community worker, or the residents' association, with much influence and their scepticism was surely correct in that there were too many uncertainties, muddles and conflicting interests for a representative view to be organised. Moreover, the community association and the worker were simply not in the business of providing leadership which might have resolved some of the issues. So residents' definitions of their situation were not significantly altered as a result of the policy change and the community-work effort. Most of the diverse interest groups defined their situation such that 'wait and see' was the predominant attitude. That broadly was still the situation in 1975. With a few exceptions, people would continue to wait and see, patching and modernising in a piecemeal way, often without improvement grants: indeed, doing what they had always done – repairing and improving as and when time and money was available. Any substantial improvement to the homes and to the environment would have to be carried out authoritatively, and with a measure of compulsion, for the local residents lacked both the resources and the confidence to force the pace.

Housing Class and Urban Management

We have described a situation in which the means of access to housing were enmeshed within a long and varied list of housing policies, none of which were communicated to residents. If we consider the diverse interests and the shared low income of the residents in the light of policies taken, then there is very little sense of the latter being informed by the former.

What was the purpose of the policy review? If the intention was to promote improvement as an alternative to clearance, then far more determined policies of improvement were necessary given the particular social structure of the locality; if, however, the intention was simply to make some marginal reduction in the redevelopment programme to save money or to minimise council involvement or the growth of public housing, then here was an ideal area in which to operate. A closer examination of what happened illustrates rather well that improvement as an *alternative* to redevelopment requires just as sweeping and effective powers as does redevelopment if, in areas of decaying landlordism and low-cost, working-class owner-occupation, there is to be any real improvement in housing and environmental conditions.

And what have been the effects? By the end of 1976, the area had a further new designation as a 'housing action area' but things looked about the same as they did in 1971 when the houses were 'saved'. Some surrounding demolition and signs of new building indicated that gradually these houses would again be part of a residential area. A few improved houses, which are owned by a housing association, the council, or one or two private owners, could be discerned by the knowing eye amidst the general shabby and worn-out mien that characterised the streets. What was their future?

Without a measure of virtual compulsion, few owners were likely to spend more than a minimum on these houses for the next few years – particularly if short-time work and inflation were to continue to reduce real wages. If progress in such areas is dependent upon energetic and well-organised participatory pressure from residents, one would predict that improvements will happen later rather than sooner. It is not inconceivable that, in a few years time, if local authorities find that they can build new houses and acquire land at economic prices rather than at today's levels of cost and interest rates, then a small patch of 100-year-old terraces may be obsolete in every way and could be demolished without pain or anguish to anyone, and in that way the original plans for comprehensive redevelopment will be fulfilled. If, however, the council actively pursues its new policy of improvement of older houses to decent standards and to manage a comprehensive improvement scheme, then these houses are a suitable case for such a treatment.

What is clear is that the future of these houses will not be determined by 'what the local people want', for the houses are inextricably linked to the housing policies of the council. If nothing much happens for ten years then that will reflect how local housing policy is managed. The shift from redevelopment to improvement did not free the houses from the influence of the council; it merely removed them from the control of one department and placed them in a sort of limbo awaiting the second coming of a saviour. So, rather literally, the decision 'saved the houses for improvement'. That improvement awaits the emergence of effective and comprehensive processes as the redevelopment process itself is forestalled. For many of the families the wait will not be pleasant, comfortable, or short, and in that respect, too, little has changed, for those were the painful characteristics of redevelopment. The surprise perhaps is the forbearance shown by the residents through the thick and the thin of it. It is probably safe to predict that such forbearance will continue to be needed for a few years to come.

Chapter 6

Case Study 4: Participation in an 'Action Area'

The Area

Our final case study is concerned with an area whose future appears to rest with the efficacy of policies by which older homes are improved and maintained with grant aid to prevent their decay and obsolescence. As our case study will show a key to the success of such policies is as much a matter of *confidence* as it is of the availability of sufficient resources; and in attaining confidence the ability of residents to participate in the replanning of the neighbourhood will play an important part. So this case study looks in detail at the attempts of residents to participate and at the effects and consequences of their participation.

The neighbourhood in question is directly to the south of the redevelopment area examined in the second case study; each is part of the same 'action area', with a different mode of urban renewal intended for each. It was built at about the same time as the redevelopment area but shows more variety in size of houses, the provision of larger gardens and fewer back terraces – particularly in those sections of the area furthest from the city centre. At the start of the research, there were

2700 dwellings including 190 council houses of modern construction. Open sites after demolition, patches of derelict terraces and some crammed and dilapidated homes made it a varied area, an in-between type of district which was neither a clear-cut slum awaiting redevelopment, nor the sort of area where a brisk market in houses and frequent house-painting and improvement indicated confidence and optimism about the future. Running down the middle of the neighbourhood is a busy shopping street, many of whose shops cater for an Asian population: small grocers and greengrocers, supermarkets and a wide variety of wholesale and retail textile businesses. Asians comprise perhaps 20 per cent of all households, and other immigrant groups – West Indian and Irish – are well represented. It is an area of uniform small houses, most of which, when our work started, were in owner-occupation but with a significant minority, perhaps 30 per cent, in privately let unfurnished tenancies.

Research–Action

The action role whereby 'data' were obtained for this case study was that of secretary to a residents' association which was established in the area expressly to enable participation in planning to occur. The secretary was not a member of the research team but a community worker already involved in 'an action setting' who had influenced the setting up of the residents' association. He had been a research worker before becoming a community worker and was familiar with the aims and content of the research project. He was commissioned, with the agreement of his association, to prepare a series of documents on his work and on the history and personnel of the association. The residents' association also agreed to make available a complete set of documents – minutes, letters and reports – pertaining to its work. As a result of this commission the secretary was enabled to work on a part-time basis as the association's secretary, and was in effect contracted to them to advise and assist their work.

The secretary approached his work with a concern to see that civil rights could be exercised and maintained and saw his role in the residents' association very much as an adviser to the group, rather similar to that of a local-authority officer who gives professional advice to his committee. He estimated that this deliberate attempt on his part to create for himself a 'professional' and technical role would ease his access to information from, and gain the confidence of, the council officers with whom he spoke. Thus he saw one of his jobs as that of interpreting planners' jargon and political possibilities to residents and interpreting residents' wishes into something usable and reasonably convincing to the city council. He recognised, however, that this style of work suited the main participants in the residents' association who were owner-occupiers either wanting General Improvement Area status for the neighbourhood and improvement grants, or requesting clearance, rehousing and compensation. Those whose demands were more in conflict with the way in which the council officers structured debate – council tenants in old acquired property seeking repairs and transfers, for instance – rarely participated in the association's activities.

In this way the insights and information provided lack representativeness and the data are of a different kind than would come from a conventional enquiry.

Our vantage point is that of an informed, involved activist who saw a scheme under way and maintained a documentary record. He did not conduct formal interviews as an impartial observer but has recorded how officials came, spoke, agreed and negotiated, how expectations on either side were expressed, fulfilled and disappointed and how a *process* was worked out for the local people involved. Very little of the information made available for the research could have been obtained except by way of this action involvement.

Participation in Outline

The main events with which we are concerned occurred in a 2½-year period spanning three public meetings called by the city council's planning committee. At the first, in April 1971, the only plans for the area were of an extremely general nature; on a large map displayed at the meeting was the legend 'To be determined' – and that was about it. At the second meeting, in September 1972, the city council presented draft proposals which went some way to meeting residents' wishes. At the third meeting, in January 1974, formal proposals were presented which were then the planning policy of the council towards this area.

In the period prior to the first meeting there was some locally organised activity. In December 1970 a local Labour councillor held a public meeting at a school hall in the area attended by about forty local residents. At that time the Conservative Party was controlling the city council and the meeting was intended to be a protest about conditions in the area. It decided to petition the council for an official public meeting and definite plans for the area.

A community worker with a local advice centre who attended that meeting subsequently organised with the full agreement of the councillor a series of street meetings which led to the formation of a neighbourhood-wide residents' association which discussed and pre-pared a programme to present to the first official public meetings. Thereafter the association remained in contact with the planning department and pressed for the resolution of certain questions in a promised draft plan for the area. From April 1972 to March 1973, dialogue, argument and consultation continued, resulting in revisions in policies along lines suggested by the residents' association. These revised proposals were ratified by the city council in December 1973 and made public at a meeting early in 1974.

These plans are the basis of a programme now under way. There will be General Improvement Areas within the district and there is a clear indication of which areas will be demolished. The residents' association provided information to support General Improvement Area de-clarations in two parts of the area and these were proposed and accepted at the 1972 meeting. However, at that meeting the planners proposed for a substantial number of houses an interim categorisation for which neither full improvement-grant aid nor a definite clearance date would be given. Between 1972 and 1973 the residents argued for the abolition of this interim category and the extension both of improvement areas and proposed clearance areas. To a great extent the arguments were accepted and incorporated in zoning proposals and a future clearance programme.

So, from uncertainty and demoralisation in 1971 the situation in 1975 was certain. A plan of action, in whose making residents had participated, was the basis for future developments in the area.

Participation Examined

The foregoing account is the bare bones of a complex process, and by 1975 there was still uncertainty on some crucial questions: Will the worst houses be demolished as promised? Who will live in the new houses when they are built? When will they be built? When will the promised environmental improvements in the General Improvement Areas be carried out?

What had been achieved was *planning* certainty. But plans are like promises. What has been exposed to the residents as a result of their association's participation is the difference between planning and action. The association members and the secretary are well aware of the limitations of their participatory success. They have been aware, as the process developed, that their success in negotiations with planners was not matched by their success in negotiations with other departments of the city council whose resources are more tangible and actual than the maps, zonings, hatchings, dots, circles, dates and terminology with which the planners made them familiar.

A rather closer examination of the process can indicate more clearly the nature of the participatory power exercised by the residents. A look at the secretary, the association and its members, their relations with relevant departments of the city council and with politicians can provide the illuminating detail.

The Role of the Secretary

At the time of the public meeting which exacted the promise of a plan, the association's secretary was employed as a community worker by a local, independent neighbourhood centre. The street meetings which had led to the founding of the association were called under the auspices of that centre, and the community worker made it clear that he was employed there. The centre's reputation in the neighbourhood was one of involvement in welfare matters and in providing legal and housing advice. It was therefore consistent with this image for the worker to be concerned with the environmental and housing issues central to the plan. The worker was not self-consciously doing 'community development' in this task, for the general approach he adopted stemmed more from a concern for civil rights and the relationships within which they are achieved. At the first collective meeting of street representatives it was moved that he be chairman. He explained that this would be wrong since he was not a local resident and it was most important for the organisation to be seen unambiguously as a *residents'* association. However, it was very clear to all present that they needed someone like the worker and he was therefore co-opted to act as secretary and adviser to the association.

The first street meetings, the numbers who came and their enthusiasm for something to be done convinced the secretary that the city council's intended policies – for rehabilitation and improvement of sound housing and only partial demolition – were relevant and in the interests of local residents. However, it was a situation in which the execution of policy depended on a combination of technical expertise and local confidence. Without the understanding and active co-operation of residents the technical requirements of the policy – getting old homes modernised – would simply not be achieved. It was clear to the secretary that the non-existent relationship between officers and local residents made co-operation unlikely. Furthermore, the popular reputation of the city council for bull-dozing, not just acres of old housing but also critics and protestors who wished to argue, limited local confidence in any plans. It was also clear that the council was not going to employ anyone to promote a new kind of relationship and understanding. This context meant that the role of secretary was crucial and that it was a complex mediating and interpreting role. This is how one of the association's members defined the work of the Secretary:

> He will be a link-man with some free time to devote to the community's affairs, encouraging the street associations and helping them to united action through the residents' association. A secretary is needed to ensure regular meetings, issue minutes, follow things up in letters and on the phone and generally keep things moving between meetings. We were lucky to get a secretary who had (a) the knowledge and experience, (b) dedication (and so we probably left too much to him!), (c) who was ready to speak our language and (d) had lots of patience and a sense of humour.

The Residents' Association

The secretary worked with the group of about twelve people which met regularly for more than three years, with relatively little change of membership. In negotiations with the city council about the plans for their area, it regarded itself as the representative body of all residents, and by and large the council seemed to recognise its legitimacy.

The association was a representative council of six street associations or groups founded between January and March 1971. Two representatives from each group formed the association, which elected its own officers. Its aim was to co-ordinate the activities of the groups and organise information and negotiations. It was never claimed that the association was a spontaneous movement of protest by the indigenous working class faced with appalling conditions or the threat of extinction through redevelopment.

In response to the Labour councillor's initiatives, the worker from the neighbourhood centre invited a small group of other workers from local voluntary organisations, a children's day centre, an adventure playground, and a neighbouring area's advice centre, as well as the councillor, to meet for discussion on how and whether local people might have a say in the plans being prepared. The councillor made it clear that he was willing to raise any matters in the council chamber and deal with any individual cases. After he had left the meeting the remainder decided that a series of street meetings should be called to see whether there was interest in forming a representative association to negotiate for 'participation'.

There were six meetings, all remarkably well attended. The smallest was of eighty people, the largest was of 250, most attracting between 100 and 150. They followed something of a pattern. The community worker would explain why the meeting had been called, that the city council was preparing plans, that the content of those plans could and should reflect the wishes of local people and it would need local people to organise and keep up the pressure so that the plans occurred sooner rather than later. At most meetings, despite the routine sceptics, racialists and jokers, committees of six or eight people were formed to explore further action. Some of these committees developed into quite formal street associations with membership dues and regular meetings; others were very informal. In time all the committees organised, with help, self-administered surveys of their area and presented the results to the main association.

The distinctly local base for these first meetings and the subsequent surveys undoubtedly aided effective organisation. When a meeting of street representatives was called in March 1971, no one disputed the idea of forming one big association for the area which would co-ordinate the exisiting small groups. This basis for membership remained throughout the next three years and was still in existence at the time of writing.

If well-attended street meetings provided the formal basis of representativeness for the association, the way in which it was actually justified is more complex and was based on a succession of activities which sustained contact between street representatives, the association and residents.

In the first place association meetings were not closed, and private affairs and street committee members were welcomed as 'visitors' able to take part as they wished. This enabled formal representation to be changed from time to time without challenging the way the association was constituted. Second, the association sought to communicate what it was doing through a free newspaper whose distribution was the responsibility of association members through their street groups. Between July 1971 and December 1973 five editions of this newspaper were produced. A further aid to representativeness were the surveys and the careful use of the evidence they produced at public meetings, in negotiations with officers and in the newspaper. The surveys were carried out by local members, ensuring actual contact between the street representatives and their neighbours.

An undoubted aid to the association's claim to representativeness was its adopted strategy at public meetings. Carefully and deliberately the association planned its public displays: it arranged discussions with residents about the content of meetings before they took place; they organised wide publicity so that there was a large audience to hear their association representatives speak about local issues with which they were familiar. The idea was for the maximum number of residents to witness and take part in an *event*, forcing the city council to take seriously what the residents said.

The first public meeting in April 1971 set the pattern for those which followed. It was significant that the council's own publicity was minimal and the councillors and officers who attended were surprised both at the turn-out and at the degree of organisation. They were clearly unprepared, for they came with detailed proposals for the adjoining redevelopment area and only the blandest and most general statements for the area of our case study. Their map merely showed the whole of this area hatched in blue with the words 'To be determined' printed over it. The residents' association was readily able to exploit the situation. If these were plans that had been promised, then it was feeble that they had nothing to say; if it really was 'to be determined' then the residents would have a say in the determination. The association was able to appear representative both to the residents and to the members and officers of the council.

There is another sense in which this representativeness was organised. It became clear to the secretary that the association members were constantly seeking to be seen as, and being referred to as, 'good representatives' by their neighbours. They knew that they could not fool their neighbours and, if there were failures, they would soon hear about them and be criticised. The members were most sensitive to occasions when they were made to look foolish in the eyes of their neighbours by communicating official assurances which subsequently were negated. Unless they could be seen to make council promises stick, then there was no point in continuing, for broken promises were the order of the past. Far more important to members than any formal legitimacy for representativeness in terms of meetings or elections was this more fragile sense of doing well by your neighbours and of not being 'conned' by the council. It was clear that neighbours did talk about the plan and the association, and gossip and rumour was important 'binding' which kept the association members both together and in touch with their areas.

What interests and views were actually being represented? The area has been described as heterogeneous in tenure, age, race and other family characteristics. Only a little of this heterogeneity was reflected in the make-up of association representatives. All but one were 'real Brummies', mostly owner-occupiers, the middle-aged male backbone of the city's working class, respectable, conservative in outlook, largely unused to participatory politics of any kind. This homogeneity certainly facilitated cohesiveness and basic agreement in objectives, but was it not inimical to a wide representation of diverse local interests? In some respects this was so; but the association was seeking to represent an area's interest in council plans. It was not a *narrow* self-interest which informed its members views. Indeed, as time went on, they realised the complexity of their demands in council policy terms. Their collective definition of a 'good area' was not in terms of uniformity, but rather in terms of *confidence*. It was therefore not enough for just the best streets to be 'saved' – they sought assurances that in 'saved' areas houses would be improved, that the worst houses would be cleared, that new houses would be built and that local residents would have the option of occupying those new homes.

Three issues can indicate, in practice, the breadth of interest expressed by the association. The first relates to the council's initial lifing proposals with houses deemed to be (i) suitable for retention within General Improvement Areas, (ii) suitable for early demolition, and (iii) an interim category, suitable for short-term retention but with no long-term lifing certainty. The association successfully opposed the last category, as it was seen to be a source of continued blight and dereliction. As a result of the decision to abolish the interim category, both General Improvement Areas and demolition areas were enlarged. But the issue illustrates the general representativeness of the association: if it simply had the interests of owner-occupiers at heart, then the council's first proposals would have sufficed since most of the obvious areas well represented by the association were included in the initial proposed General Improvement Areas.

The second issue concerns the various interests as represented by different racial groups. The area is multiracial and, although the initial street meetings, street committees and public meetings reflected this, after the first few meetings the association's representatives have all been white. The association saw to it that its 'News' contained some lines in Asian languages directing those interested to the neighbourhood centre, though largely leaving it up to the centre to communicate the plan and proposals to the Asian population. In general terms they believed that the line they proposed to the council about improvement rather than redevelopment was consistent with the interests of many Asian and West Indian families whom they knew to be keen and energetic owner-occupiers. Indeed, there was no indication that the local grape-vine precluded Asian and West Indian residents.

However, the situation in those parts of the area which were to be demolished was quite different, and here the association was partisan, albeit in an unaggressive manner. In these areas there was considerable division of opinion: typically the white residents were tenants of private landlords and wanted demolition as soon as possible so that they could be rehoused by the city council. Generally, conditions in the areas were such that landlords treated them as areas for eventual demolition and spent a minimum on maintenance and repair. The immigrant families, however, tended to be owners who may well have been ill-advised to buy the houses and found them impossible to repair at reasonable expense and discovered that no grant aid was available. However, in terms of weekly costs, the houses were cheap and the council-house alternative was relatively more costly and this was an important factor for families who were sending quite substantial cash to other members of the family back home. Many therefore wanted the houses to remain and felt that compulsory take-over by the council was unnecessary interference. The neighbourhood centre found itself advising some groups of those owners about how to petition for special cases to be made by the council. The residents' association, however, was satisfied that the houses should be demolished.

Far more problematic than the immigrant groups were the 'problem families'. It would have been very easy for the residents' association, given its interests and style, to share and amplify the popular view that the main reason for the area's decline was the presence of certain families forced on them as tenants of short-life council houses. It was a commonly held opinion that the policy of using such housing for families with a record of rent arrears, vandalism, disorder and nuisance was destructive of the confidence necessary for plans for area and house improvement. However, the association did not campaign for their removal; anyway, such views tended to be voiced in the same breath by those who attributed the decline of the area to 'immigrants'. Rather, the association saw that the continuation of the 'tenure' – short-life council houses – was the problem. They therefore sought early demolition and instant closing of the worst houses, argued against the maintenance of a 'short-term retention' housing category and stressed the need for local rehousing both in improved older housing and in new council units. The association also vigorously tackled the housing department's rudimentary policy on maintenance to acquired property, seeking, if anything, to improve conditions in the short-life houses and to tackle the longer-term problem by working on the plan that was being prepared.

These three issues found the association avoiding any narrow representation of owner-occupiers engaged simply in extending the availability of improvement-grant aid in the area. Indeed, few, if any, of the members seemed to be interested in the improvement in their capital asset which the plan would bring. The plan was not seen merely in terms of bringing material improvements to the physical stock – the interest and attachment to the area seemed to go deeper.

Consistent with the association's representative approach was its dominant style of operation. As representatives they asked to be treated seriously and behaved conscientiously with that expectation. Sober negotiation, polite letters and careful displays at meetings and to the press were the order of the day. More flamboyant tactics were never seriously considered. Demonstrations, street plays, techniques of shock, shame or mockery, or even of despairing insistence for attention, would have been rejected by the members and would not have made sense to their neighbours. It was essentially and deliberately a *responsible* style of operation; thus, it was hoped, a 'responsible' policy (which the association believed improvement to be) might result.

The Association and the City Council

The association, soundly organised, confident of its neighbourhood base and serviced by an experienced community worker with informal access to most sources of relevant professional advice (town planners, surveyors, lawyers and architects), was in business to influence what plans were made by the city council for the area. The bulk of its contact – informal meetings, letters, telephone calls and formal meetings – was with officers of the planning and redevelopment section of the public works department and the then city engineer, who, as head of that department, was also the council's chief planning officer. As time went by, contact was also had with other officials, from public health, housing, estates and salvage departments, and latterly with officers given responsibility for the city's new urban renewal policy, formulated in 1972.

In March 1971 the community worker had a time-table of events in his mind, derived from his informal contacts in the planning and redevelopment section of the public works department. In April the residents' association would receive outline land-use plans and a time-table for the implementation of 'action-area' proposals from the planning section. These would be the subject of a public meeting in the area which would be followed by a flurry of consultation, argument and revision to allow final and agreed plans to be approved within six months and would lead to a start on the long process of implementation from 1972 onwards. In reply to the councillor's petition, the chairman of the public works committee had said that plans were being prepared and there would be a meeting. All indications pointed to an April meeting, prior to the May election, and prior to possible changes in the political control of the city council and delays which would follow during a period of handover (in fact, the Conservatives did not lose control to Labour until May 1972).

The public meeting was held by the city council in April 1971. Although the association had, at its first meeting, sent a letter to the chairman of the public works committee asking about the date of the meeting, and, though a polite reply was received to the effect that a decision would be made that very week, neither the association nor the neighbourhood centre was informed. Fortunately, however, the community worker spotted a small official notice in an evening newspaper and the association had a week in which to organise. Not only had the city council given very short notice, they provided minimal publicity and had called the meeting in a fairly small church hall; the association was not impressed and responded in attacking mood.

The association's hopes for a large turnout were more than fulfilled, with many more people coming to the hall than could be seated. The sizeable posse of council dignitaries, chairman and officers, were obviously surprised, though it was not clear whether they were pleased. The audience was also surpirsed and, initially, dismayed to find no plans for their area but detailed plans for the adjoining redevelopment part of the 'action area'. A subsequent show of hands found that only six persons from the redevelopment area were present. All that was provided on the map was a clear boundary and the words 'To be determined'. The planners spoke of a 'feasibility study' for the area. In a summary of this report, which was supplied to the association, it was stated that the neighbourhood:

> comprises areas of housing which are the subject of clearance action at present and others which are likely to be included within clearance areas shortly. There are some houses with a life of at least twenty years and the majority of houses have an anticipated life of between ten and twenty years. A plan of part development and part redevelopment is therefore proposed. This would involve the acquis- ition of further properties in addition to those already in Corporation ownership and those acquired under the clearance provision of the Housing Acts. The proposals . . . envisage the closure of certain roads and new roadworks; the provision of open space and smaller amenity areas; public car parks and off street parking facilities; and the provision of other facilities which are at present lacking. A further report . . . will be submitted at a later date.

It was hardly surprising in view of this that the chairman of the public meeting tried to steer discussion to the proposals for the adjoining area. The association's spokesman, however, insisted that he and his colleagues would focus on their area. The large audience heard the association's chairman and secretary report on the results of their own brief surveys; how the majority of people were in favour of staying in an improved area, that they did not want large-scale redevelopment, that there were obvious needs for improvements to schools, shops, play facilities, parking and traffic as well as to the houses and that this should happen quickly. Council chairmen expressed their general agreement and the city engineer and planning officer spoke of 'technical co- operation' between his officers and the association and promised a detailed plan within twelve months. It was also agreed that the emphasis in the plan should be on rehabilitation and improvement rather than demolition.

From the association's point of view, the meeting could hardly have been more successful, and if a year for a detailed plan sounded a long time then at least the promise of formal consultation had been made. An anxious chairman of the public works committee had sought to assure association members after the meeting that 'We're all on the same side, really, you know.'

As a result of this meeting the secretary made contact with members of the planning section dealing with the plan, and formal communication with the chief officer was established on an apparently cordial basis. The team actually dealing with the plan was very small – two people – and it had responsibility for planning exercises in the whole of the inner ring. Most of the section at this time were preoccupied with the structure plan and its head was on loan to the regional study team.

It soon appeared that the planners were greatly constrained by assessments of lifing for properties made by the public health department. Although they, the planners, were 'for' improvement, they felt it would prove very difficult to get General Improvement Area status for many of the houses. Those which the public health inspector had lifed for twenty years and more were possible candidates, but there were many houses which were irretrievably doomed for demolition and there was a large group of houses lifed between ten and twenty years and for which a policy needed to be marked out.

The association tried to establish contact with the public health department, because the chief public health and housing inspector had a reputation for being 'for improvement' and because of the clear power of his department in the process of improvement. The attitudes and expectancies of the *local* public health inspectors, however, were found to be opposed to improvement. Undoubtedly sincere in their attitudes, tempered by many years of policing the slums, they were typified by the claim that 'we inspectors have been dealing with old houses all our lives and we know when it is no longer worth prolonging their lives'. Such an attitude was hardly conducive to further liaison and the attempt to work with the local inspectorate was virtually abandoned at the outset.

Progress was slow, and by the autumn of 1971 the association had become impatient and lobbied hard with councillors and their M. P.; an article in a professional journal at this time may also have helped its case with council officers. Eventually, following a letter from the chief planning officer in which possible General Improvement Area designations within the neighbourhood were mentioned, a meeting for association representatives was arranged for December. The association responded positively, offering co-operation 'in creating the means to implement such a policy fully'.

The meeting was called by the chief planning officer, but it was the chief public health and housing inspector who invited the association to test the feasibility of General Improvement Areas in two sections of the area. It was explained that the houses within these areas were the only ones which could be given G. I. A. status, such being only possible where most properties had a life of at least fifteen years. At its meeting the association agreed to survey all households in the two areas and to provide the information to the planning section by January 1972. It agreed to keep the information confidential for the time being, but pressed the section to include clear lifing proposals for *all* houses in its plans. At the December meeting the chief planning officer had said that the plan would be ready by April.

The association fulfilled its promise about the surveys and the information was with the planners early in February. The surveys indicated overwhelming support for the proposed improvement areas. Confident that in the spring of 1972 the second public meeting (promised at the April 1971 meeting) would take place, the association relaxed a little and took up some non-housing issues with other departments. The chief planning officer had submitted a 'preliminary report and policy statement' which was approved by his committee, and there was no party-political dispute over its contents. In the event the public meeting was delayed until September (partly caused by the local elections at which the Labour Party took control of the city council); meanwhile the 'preliminary report and policy statement' was carefully studied by the association. The report is a highly significant document in that it indicates the way 'participation' had gone for the city council. Only its introduction and summarising sections, 'policy statement – planning objectives', were circulated to residents for discussion, though the association's secretary acquired a full report whose contents were made known to association members well before the meeting.

For a document which took a year to prepare it is exceedingly thin, bland and generalised. It would seem that it took longer to achieve interdepartmental consultations about the necessity for a report than it did to discuss and prepare the report itself. The report included a section on 'liaison' with the association which summarised, without comment, criticism or support, what the association's surveys indicated. No discussion of aims and objectives, no indications of whether what was proposed was consistent with residents' wishes, and no suggestion that future liaison might be valuable, were to be found. The most important part of the report was on lifing of property and was contained in a plan 'prepared with the agreement of the Public Health and Housing Departments' and defined for discussion purposes:

(1) Those areas suggested to the Health Committee for General Improvement Action.
(2) Dwellings of modern construction to be retained.
(3) Older dwellings to be retained.
(4) Properties affected by road widening.
(5) Properties to be subject to clearance action.

The report also contained an implicit time-table with a ten-year programme including acquisition and clearance of unfit and non-conforming properties within the first seven years and demolition of 1200 properties between 1975 and 1977.

This time-table and the lifing plans were the planning section's attempt to get the housing issues resolved so as to allow detailed planning to proceed. It is significant that about 50 per cent retention and 50 per cent demolition were being proposed; but there was considerable opacity about the form of retention for the 550 older dwellings not in proposed general improvement areas. The proposed timing was also extraordinarily vague. No dates were given to G. I. A. declarations; there was no indication about when a planning compulsory-purchase order might be made, and publicity at this time suggested that the process was exceedingly cumbersome and long-winded. Only vague hints were made that housing compulsory-purchase orders, which were quicker, might be prepared. References to ten years and seven years indicated the fundamental uncertainty of the process.

The association discussed the report in April and sent some initial observations to officers and councillors, seeking an early public meeting. In May a series of street meetings was organised at which the proposals were discussed in detail so that the association could represent area views at the public meeting. A series of six questions was sent to chairmen and chief officers of relevant council committees in advance of the meeting to ensure that full answers could be given.

The platform at the public meeting in September consisted of the chairmen of public works, housing and health committees, the chief

planning officer, the chief public health and housing inspector, a senior
official for the housing department and a senior official for the estates
department. Also on the platform was the chairman of the newly
formed 'standing conference on urban renewal', which was the Labour-
controlled council's base for a new initiative for areas of older property.

Opening the meeting the chairman of the public works committee
stressed that it was a draft plan, it could be altered and that was why the
meeting had been called: 'Your views are welcome, we will take them
into consideration where it is practicable, and it is not always possible,
but obviously sympathetic consideration will be given to your views.'
He commented briefly on the questions submitted, reckoning that he
agreed with most points and the possibilities would be explored.

The association's chairman started off discussion from the floor
saying that the association could claim to have reached and speak for
probably 65 – 70 per cent of the population. He said that the contact
over the last eighteen months had been valuable but progress was slow.
He referred to the *Evening Mail*, which had spoken about residents
giving the planners an ultimatum:

> I don't know what the editor means by this. There is very little that
> we can do that we have not already done. If an ultimatum means
> what will be the result of actions *not* being taken, Mr Chairman, I can
> tell you: if action is not taken and taken immediately – you will have
> one of the finest and fastest slums in Birmingham within twelve
> months.

He went on to the plan's reference to partial redevelopment over ten
years:

> Ten years is half a generation. In ten years' time the young men of
> this area will be middle-aged. In ten years' time the middle-aged will
> be old. In ten years' time the old people won't want an improved
> house, they will want a little plot in Brandwood End [the local
> cemetery]. Speed is the essence of the contract.

His speech was clapped and cheered by the audience, further
establishing the legitimacy of the association. The secretary then rose to
introduce the association's six points and to hear the answers. The six
points were:

(1) Could there not be General Improvement Area treatment for those houses designated 'to be retained'?

(2) Could not the city council press for a wider interpretation of improvement grants to cover items of general repair?

(3) Could the council have a clear plan for cleared sites between demolition and rebuilding to prevent them becoming rubbish-tips?

(4) What assurances could the council give that fair compensation would be paid to owners and tenants who looked after their houses well, but which were in demolition areas?

(5) How was the council going to phase demolition and rebuilding? What time-table and what policy assurances could be given on local rehousing?

(6) Could the proposed demolition areas be reconsidered? Many people would be prepared to improve their houses if grants were obtainable and if assurances could be given.

These points had been already the subject of informal discussions with the local planning team and with other officials, but informal contact had merely succeeded in communicating these issues and had not achieved any assurances. This was why the issues were presented with such a critical and demanding style at the meeting. The replies were far more positive than had been indicated informally. Assurances were given that detailed surveys for extending improvement areas would be made and areas scheduled for demolition would be reconsidered.

The chairman of the new standing conference on urban renewal provided some definite information on a new policy for cleared sites. The least satisfactory answers were provided on issues of compensation and rehousing policy. But the main message to come over was that the lifing of properties would be reviewed and that co-operation would continue. The question of speed and timing was resolutely stonewalled by all the platform speakers, who stressed the uncertainty and the slow rate of the over-all process. No assurances were given about speeding the exercise up.

The meeting illustrated the peak of the association's influence with the planning section. The eighteen months of negotiations had clearly established the primacy of lifing for the future planning of the area. During the negotiations the association had carefully not countered, challenged or criticised the lifing proposals. Only when they became public at the meeting, did the association press for changes. The

informal contacts had suggested that whatever the planners thought
they were not the most important decision-makers about lifing and
timing. The kinds of proposals made by the planners – especially in the
report – were cautious and conservative, reflecting almost nothing at
all of the pressure, contact, communication and urgency which had
characterised the association's approach.

Two other points raised at the public meeting were never satisfactorily resolved. In both cases other departments were concerned and the
failure to achieve mutually acceptable policies highlights the failure to
co-ordinate plans and policies for the neighbourhood.

· The first of these was *the rehousing issue.* Contact with the housing
department on the subject of local rehousing for residents affected by
clearance was mainly in the year after the September meeting. The
chairman of the housing committee had been sympathetic, and the
housing department officer at the meeting referred to a block of new
housing which was mainly occupied by local people. Following the
meeting the officer offered to come and discuss the matters with the
association, and this was arranged. The association prepared a note
outlining some ideas about how local participation might improve the
policies: a well-communicated register of local housing, a register of
local needs and a definite policy of priority for local people displaced by
clearance. Moreover, and crucial for the confidence which the
association sought to build up, it suggested an interim use of old houses
for *local* families seeking a stay in the area until a new house was
available. It also made proposals for 'good-neighbour schemes', clear
phasing and a swiftly administered scheme of rehousing and demolition.

The official came and discussed the document. He tried to leave the
impression with the association that few of their ideas were practicable,
that the housing department did a difficult job well, people were housed
in the area they asked for and only the most marginal changes in policy
were necessary. He was given a fairly rough time by the association,
which indicated most clearly why confidence was non-existent between
his department and local residents. But he conceded nothing and gave
no assurances, appearing eager and confident to do a public-relations
job for his department. In that he failed miserably. He simply
convinced the association that, in the future, on housing issues, they
must seek the support and influence of their councillors, their M. P. and
seek to discuss policy at the committee chairman level.

This proved exceedingly difficult. The local Labour M. P. enthusiastically supported the idea of a full discussion between the chairman of the housing committee and the residents' association about the need for a policy on local rehousing. But it seemed that his support got nowhere with the chairman. The approach started in March; nothing had happened by May, when the chairman apologised that due to the election he was unavailable. Soon after he was hospitalised and then convalescent, and it was not until August that his deputy agreed to a meeting and at such short notice that the M.P. was unable to attend. However, the meeting merely confirmed that neither the chairman nor his deputy could see that there was a policy issued beyond confirming that, wherever possible, people were rehoused in their area of choice and, if they asked to be rehoused locally, they would be. The deputy chairman at the August meeting was quite aggressively emphatic that there was no role for the association in policy discussions on housing and little of value in the association's ideas.

Formally, the matter rested there and was most unsatisfactory from the association's point of view. It was no great reassurance to them to hear that the official who came to meet them had issued an instruction to his staff to ensure local rehousing wherever possible. The association did not want a succession of individual favours at the time of rehousing; it wanted a clear time-tabled programme which organised local rehousing and gave residents confidence in the administrative processes.

The other important issue raised at the public meeting was of compensation for owners of houses acquired by the council. An official of the estates department, which manages matters of valuation and compensation, was questioned about a recently publicised case of a man who was offered compensation in 1972 for a well-built, well-decorated home which was *less* than the council's mortgage valuer had approved four years before. The association's spokesman raised the issue of the way the slum-clearance procedure artificially depressed values which then became the guidelines for compensation, such that compensation bore little relation to the actual cost of similar alternative houses in areas where clearance was not proposed. This could force people into a situation of having to accept a council tenancy. The official declined to speak on an individual case and was surprised at the laughter which greeted his remark when he said that only very few householders were disappointed with the compensation they received.

The matter of compensation was raised again early in 1973, resulting in a courteous explanation to the secretary of the complexities of valuation practice, levels of compensation and policy on prices paid for properties acquired before compulsory-purchase procedures were completed. On one special case brought to the attention of the association, the department acknowledged an error and remitted the situation by arranging a correct offer. Again, it appeared that the association had no way of proceeding on the larger issue, which ran counter to professional practice, and until actual cases started to be dealt with there was little for an association to do.

After the public meeting, however, some progress was certainly made. The association encouraged objections from individuals in the parts of the area zoned for clearance so that the promised review could take place, it encouraged and assisted one street association to prepare a detailed case for a further G. I. A. declaration and it pressed for extension of G. I. A. boundaries. When a revised plan was approved in April 1973, the interim category of housing to be retained but not included in G. I. A.s was removed; the whole area was declared for either demolition or as eligible for full improvement-grant aid. The significant person in this decision appeared to be the chief planning officer, though it certainly reflected the drift in the city council and government thinking on the subject.

While the association was engaged in 'technical co-operation' with the planners, in pressing for environmental improvements and for policies on rehousing, allocations and compensations, it also had to deal with a constant stream of troubles about the frequency and efficiency of rubbish collections, street-cleaning, pavement repairs and tipping on cleared sites. While the planners liked to conceive of area improvement in terms of paved areas, play spaces, shopping precincts and 'street furniture', the most common wish for local people for area improvement concerned the improvement of rubbish collection.

The association sought a policy on dustbin provision and considered that, if families were large and collections irregular, a second bin was a necessity. Policy, however, was hard to find as public health and salvage departments conferred and squabbled. Eventually the salvage department did confirm a policy that was, on paper, satisfactory to the association; in practice, however, most association members concluded that, whatever was officially declared policy, a tip to the dustmen was the best way.

From April 1973 momentum on the plan was lost. The association's secretary was informed informally that draft zoning proposals (the final formal stage in 'action-area' planning) had been made but had only got as far as a senior planning officer's desk drawer. They remained there for three months and it was not until October 1973 that the planning section finally approved a detailed plan which was subsequently made public in January 1974 at another meeting in the area.

At the September 1972 meeting, the chairman of the urban renewal conference had impressed the audience with his stress on real issues, his candid acknowledgement of past mistakes and his hopes for the future. He referred to plans for thirty-seven empty sites in the city needing attention, nine of which were in the area in question. He was as good as his word and so it was with positive feelings that the association had sent representatives to a meeting at the Council House in January 1973 to hear about the council's new urban renewal policy. It sounded rather like a list of the association's requests and demands over the past four years and gave the association some hopes that communication and co-ordination would greatly improve and that this plan, once approved, would be acted upon. The first signs were encouraging. Some cleared sites were grassed over, information was plentiful and an officer from the architect's department started coming to association meetings and was setting up plans for discussing the contents of the environmental improvements in the proposed General Improvement Areas. However, early hopes were not fulfilled; the architect was whisked away to other areas and other factors have entered to add to the delay and inaction in implementing the plan. Some of these other factors are referred to in a postscript to this study.

What needs to be stressed here is that the association's relations with various officers and councillors were a various patchwork of hostility, apprehension, positive interest and genuine respect and appreciation. The net effect was that despite the association's wish for speed continued delays were met. The irony is that so often participation is blamed for holding up planning and decision-making, and yet here is a case where the organisation and administration of the processes of change militated against the residents' wish for speed! It is perhaps worth recalling that it was in April 1971 that the first meeting occurred and it took until January 1974 for a plan to exist publicly and formally as a guide for city council action. 'Speed,' as the Chairman of the Association had said in that burst of optimism in September 1972, 'is the essence of the contract.'

The Association and the Elected Representatives

In 1971, when the story began, in local political terms the neighbourhood of this case study was in a 'marginal' ward, represented by one Labour councillor and two Conservatives. This might have led one to suppose that there would be very considerable interest in the activities of a well-organised local residents' association.

In December 1970 it was the Labour councillor who called the initial public meeting, in response to which the neighbourhood worker (who later became the secretary) initiated his activities. It should be remembered that at this time it was assumed that the plan would be finalised within six months, and initially there was no thought of organising a longer-term involvement – just hopes that a successful 'run' on the plan would lead to other more interesting and long-term concerns in which the association could become involved.

The Labour councillor attended some of the street meetings but rarely spoke or took an active part. One street association invited one of the Conservative councillors to a meeting and the main association also had one meeting with him.

The association itself, though, carefully sought to be non-party political and discouraged any identification with local councillors. The association's chairman was a long-standing Conservative Party member and the first vice-chairman was a Labour Party activist, but both agreed that the association should avoid a party label.

The Labour Party took the two other ward seats from the Conservatives in May 1971. The plan was not much of an issue and what election activity there was tended to occur in other parts of the ward. Thereafter, only the original Labour councillor retained interest in and contact with the association and the local plan.

The relationship between the association and councillors was not so much an expression of a deliberately planned strategy as a response to a very common undercurrent of frustation at years of apparent neglect by the city council. Residents had come to expect very little of their councillors and the majority never bothered to vote at elections. Councillors, quite simply, were not viewed as being powerful or as having any significant influence on the city council and those who controlled it. Indeed, there existed a cynical view that asserted that local councillors were by and large waiting and jockeying for their turn to earn a place of real power as member or chairman of one of the big committees. Councillors would not publicly challenge the city council, and that was why an association needed independence from them.

To the Association the local councillors seemed little interested in being direct representatives of the area, but rather regarded themselves as elected to create and defend city government. None sought to use, control, sway or direct the association. There were no complaints from them that the association was going direct to officials, departments and committee chairmen for direct action and attention to their problems rather than using them as their spokesmen.

The Labour councillor's willingness to communicate individual complaints was the *routine* way of organising local representation, and no councillor seemed to think that it should be any other way. Thus the association used councillors for very limited purposes – to deal with individual problems when all that was needed was greater efficiency from some department in a regular activity and where no question of policy was involved.

There were, however, some other instances which did find the councillor willing and able to do more. In September 1971 the association found they had met a seeming impasse and sent a stern and exasperated letter to committee chairmen, chief officers, councillors and M. P.s seeking more action. The councillor raised the matter in the council chamber and read out the whole of the association's letter. The Labour Party was in opposition at the time so this publicity against the Conservative administration served its ends. A year and a half later, when the association was finding it difficult to discuss the rehousing issue, the councillor was contacted again; he approached the chairman of the housing committee and called a meeting, but this time he did not even come. From the outset he declined to get involved in disputes over policy – that was not a local councillor's job. So, as most of the association's concern was with broad issues of policy, the basis for a close working relationship between the association and the elected members was extremely limited.

The association members were quite clear that their matter was a *local* issue, the concern of the city council and not a matter for Parliament, and thus not one which would involve them with their M. P. On two issues, however, the association found itself liaising with the M. P. – in the first instance by accident, the second by design. Neither, however, gave any reason to believe that there was much that the M. P. could actually do. The area was affected by electoral boundary changes and was the responsibility, between elections, of the Labour M. P. for an adjoining constituency – he was a man extremely experienced in local politics both as a councillor in a large industrial city and as a serving cabinet or shadow cabinet member.

The first instance concerned the use of small sites and minor environmental works. Association members met the M. P. when they went to see their councillor at one of his 'surgeries' and found it was the evening of the M. P.'s regular monthly advice bureau for constituents. He agreed to add his support to the councillor's in the form of a letter to the chief officer of the relevant department. After about one month the members visited the bureau again to find that there had been no response. The M. P. again wrote a forceful and supporting letter which asked for action and comment, sending the association a copy and promising further contact. Soon after there were some signs of pavement repairs being done – but they never heard further on the matter either from the M. P. or from the department concerned. For the association the issue was a first instance of the city council's extremely limited capacity and willingness to co-operate and indicated also that not much notice was taken of M. P. 's letters.

This incident took place when the Conservatives controlled the council. In March 1973 the association decided to launch a new attack on the rehousing issue following the unsatisfactory meeting with the senior housing committee, seeking a meeting to discuss its own policy document; letters were also sent to councillors and to the M. P. of the existing constituency as well as to the M. P. in whose constituency the area would be in the future. The Conservative M. P. wrote back expressing interest but nothing more and referred to the future boundary changes. The Labour M. P. was swift and emphatic in his support. He replied by letter saying how the policy document 'represents views with which I have the greatest sympathy', enclosing a copy of a letter he had sent to the housing committee chairman. He requested a meeting with the chairman at which the association should be represented. 'I am sure,' he wrote, 'that [the housing chairman] will agree to my request.' That was in April 1973. In May the Chairman sent a letter apologising for not answering but promising attention after the May elections. The M. P. also wrote back apologising for no action but assuring the association of his continuing efforts. In June the association wrote again to both asking about progress – and again in July when it also sought the interest of councillors and other departments. In August the chairman wrote back suggesting a date at the end of the month for the meeting. The M. P. was notified of the date rather than invited and was given insufficient notice to change a speaking engagement in another town. The meeting, as noted in an earlier section, found the housing chairman and officials quite unsympathetic to the association's proposals. After the meeting the M. P. still seemed keen to help and arranged to meet association members to discuss further possibilities but that meeting had to be cancelled due to the M. P. 's urgent commitments at a party conference. The meeting never took place and the majority of association members were unimpressed with his explanations and apologies and lost interest in seeking his support.

The association came to the conclusion that local Labour leaders were no more willing to respond to a Labour M. P. than had been the Conservatives. In their work with Birmingham's council leaders, as had been the case with local councillors, it seemed that even their M. P. had but limited capacity to lend powerful support.

Participation: a Postscript

The participatory negotiations we have discussed took place between January 1971 and January 1974. The plan which emerged had only a vague ten-year timing but it was due to start in 1975. It was presumed by the association that there was some sort of priority for the neighbourhood and what was happening in the area was the basis for a new style of management for urban renewal. This feeling was confirmed in 1973 when the new Labour council announced its urban renewal policy for areas of older housing between the redevelopment areas of the inner city and the suburbs. With considerable press publicity this new approach stressed both residents' participation as a keynote and also the creation of a new organisation to deal with the policy. The city council invited a large number of interested parties (including representatives of the association) to a meeting at the Council House to hear about the new plans. With some satisfaction association representatives heard about policies and proposals with which they were familiar: consultation about improvement areas and demolition areas, a new interim use for small cleared sites, a special fund for short-term environmental improvements, better street lights and street-cleaning. Also expressed were hopes for a co-ordinated approach to neighbourhood planning and candid admissions that, in the past, wishes of local people had been ignored. The message was that all this would change. Association representatives took an opportunity to welcome the new policy and report how consultations had been effective in their area, though there were some important issues which needed thorough rethinking.

Soon after this meeting the association's area, in common with the other 'renewal areas' which the council had designated, was circulated with 'white' or 'pink' letters informing residents whether their house was safe for improvement (white) or likely to be demolished (pink). A series of meetings was launched in 'renewal areas' publicising the policy. The public meeting for the association's area was managed in conjunction with a final formal public meeting setting out the city council's approved zoning proposals for the area. Spokesmen for the urban renewal policy at that meeting were cautious when handling questions about timing, stressing the scale and complexity of the new plans and indicating that there was still a chance for some demolition areas to be saved for improvement if residents so wished.

As part of the urban renewal policy administration, an architect approached the association to discuss preliminaries for environmental improvements in the General Improvement Areas; also, a different set of officers started to visit homes and discuss with residents, sometimes at street meetings, how improvement might be commenced.

All of this should have been good news for the association, and would have been if it had meant the start of implementation for the plan whose proposals they had influenced. Unfortunately it did not. The architect disappeared after a few weeks to work in another area. The new officers appeared to take things back to square one when discussing the scope for improvement with residents. There was no sign of any compulsory-purchase process which would enable demolition and rebuilding to start in 1975 or 1976.

Early in 1975 it became apparent that the new urban renewal policy was seeking to drastically reduce the council's slum-clearance proposals and to encourage improvement. However, this was a time of rising costs, inflation, unemployment and financial uncertainty and the take-up of improvement grants was therefore minimal. In the association's area just the few houses taken over from a private landlord by a housing association have been improved; otherwise there has been little sign of change, though house prices in the area have been sustained, particularly in the areas which will eventually be the subject of improvement-area action. Of more importance in view of the planning proposals, no start has been made either on demolition or on new building or on the planned proposals for neighbourhood improvement, and the last two depended upon an early demolition programme.

The association continued to meet regularly. There seemed to be less priority attached to the association's area, and the timing of future proposals became unclear. Other statutory devices appeared – for instance, housing action areas which shifted attention to other parts of the city. In the end, it seemed that the association's main contribution in three years had been to inform and involve local people in plans which, once made, were virtually redundant. That activity kept local people from thorough demoralisation and made some aware of the ways in which local government works. Four years after what initially had been conceived as a short and sharp piece of participatory lobbying, very little had changed. Looking ahead, it is hard to see where change will come in the next four years. When the planners spoke vaguely of a ten-year plan, they were being cautious but realistic, for as our story shows they, the planners, had little actual influence on the course of events in the neighbourhood. Ten years in the life of a local authority or a planning department may not be long. However, as the association's chairman said at the public meeting:

> Ten years is half a generation. In ten years' time the young men of this area will be middle-aged. In ten years' time the middle-aged will be old. In ten years' time the old people won't want a new or improved house, they will want a little plot in Brandwood End.

Some Conclusions

Participation is in many respects a corner-stone of pluralist assumptions about the nature of power and of the state in the social democracies of Western capitalism. In the final chapter we will seek to draw out the wider significance of this case-study examination of one participatory episode. What we have tried to depict is the way that interests that were widely held, articulately expressed, apparently consistent with the aims of policy, failed to gain advance while seeming to do so. The relationship between the managers and the managed did not alter during the process. 'Technical co-operation' with the planners meant influence over the formal content of formal plans. Crucial questions about resources and priorities were resolved elsewhere. Immediate concerns about living conditions, the use of houses, the protection of the neighbourhood and the preservation of community, so real and concrete for residents, were vague and abstract implications of policies and processes for administrators. The two sides scarcely met: where a focused discussion did occur – as with housing officials – the power of the latter expressed itself as intransigent and unyielding. As time went by these old cues of 'no change' became more insistent. The future of the area would be decided by 'them'; the best that local people could expect was favours – dependency and powerlessness characterised the relationship.

Do we discover here those in a common housing market situation seeking to organise as a class to further their interests and failing to do so? Here was a situation in which, despite great variety of housing positions – owners, tenants, council tenants – there was a considerable agreement about what policy should be. But crucially the capacity to turn this potentially desirable residential area into one in reality was beyond the economic means of the majority of residents. Few enjoyed opportunities for mobility: better houses elsewhere were too costly; tenants relied on the route to decent housing by way of council allocation or council redevelopment. Their present housing position reflected their relative economic position, and their power and powerlessness seems more properly an expression of that position, not of their housing position. Such rights and opportunities they possessed for bettering their situation were highly individualsied and few related directly to present housing position, but to other factors and criteria – like earning capacity, savings, years resident in the city, etc. A notion of housing class seems misplaced for this area, as for our other case-study areas; access to desirable housing lay through the web of local-authority control. The willingness of the local authority to deliver what was desired was in this instance highly questionable. The extent to which this was a matter of choice is a main theme of the concluding chapter.

Chapter 7

The State and the Housing Question

Our four case studies have been concerned with a brief period in one city's involvement with the housing question. In this concluding chapter we will seek to point out significant common themes from the four studies and suggest how they may indicate general features of the situation rather than merely applying to Birmingham. We will do this with reference to those theoretical considerations outlined in the first chapter.

On the Idea of 'Housing Class'

As we indicated in Chapter 1, the original formulation by Rex and Moore of the concept of 'housing class' was in terms of six or seven tenurial categories of present housing position which, it was claimed, could tell us something about a person's power relative to the 'means of housing'. For Rex, 'men in the same labour market may come to have differential degrees of access to housing'; this differential access 'tells us something of the potential basis for conflict' and of social organisation (Rex, 1968, p. 217).

Our studies, however, demonstrate most clearly that *present* housing situation is an extremely poor indicator of access, supporting that cogent criticism by Haddon that Rex's use of tenure categories confuses use of housing with its disposal. Power in a market derives from having something to dispose. The only 'housing classes' with something to dispose are owner-occupiers and landlords. There is little sense of market power in relation to housing observable in our case studies, and we have demonstrated, we think, the extraordinary complex sorts of access existing which cut across varieties of tenure categories. Pahl's attempted reformulation in terms of the ownership of sufficient capital confirms the market nature of housing access, but, as he acknowledges, does not cope with the large public sector. Our studies demonstrate that such was the extent of local- and central-government 'interference' in the housing market that for many families, just as present housing situation in terms of tenure was no indicator of future housing position, neither was ownership of capital. Housing opportunities, whether for mobility or improvement, were bureaucratically defined.

In our case studies the diversity of housing interests became a recurring theme; in the small area saved for improvement there were found to be extremely diverse attitudes and capacities towards improvement, diverse attachments to the present housing situation and very little basis in either the housing situation or the ownership of capital (savings) for forms of collective organisation. In the redevelopment area the minutiae of the administrative process produced similar diversity in terms of access to future housing; in the action area an effective form of organisation was apparent which combined those of diverse capital means and housing tenures in a collective definition of common interests for the neighbourhood. And in the study devoted to allocation policies we have tried to depict just how complex are the bureaucratic rules giving access to council housing.

What was common in these various situations was that most residents shared in a fundamental sense a common class position. All were workers or retired or redundant workers who sold their labour for a weekly wage or received a fixed benefit. Some, a section of the working class, could, by virtue of thrift, fortune and perhaps marginally higher wages, buy a house where and of the sort they wanted. Others could afford to improve their houses to a higher standard. A few could leave our areas to more prosperous districts nearer the suburbs. Most, however, would remain or become council tenants as that prospect was their only chance of decent housing. The housing opportunities of the overwhelming majority were critically determined by the complexity of state provision and its inadequacy, slowness and inefficiency. The common experiences of those queueing for a council flat, dependent superficially on the rate of allocation but more fundamentally on the rate of house-building, or those waiting in a condemned house for clearance and rehousing and affected by city-wide housing needs and a failure to build, or those in old housing awaiting improvements from an overworked, financially restricted, and in some ways powerless, bureaucracy, all seemed to confirm and sustain the collective class position of most of the inner-city residents we met. There seemed nothing 'independent' or 'autonomous' about their housing situation. It seemed a direct reflection of their position in the class structure of contemporary capitalist society.

There were complex differences in use and exchange values, in power and access in the housing market, and in the system of allocation, which are interesting and worthy of explanation, but it is wrong to compare these complexities with differences in *class* position. It says nothing more about the situation of a stoker and his family who rent a furnished room and that of a bus driver's family, who are also private tenants, to say that they share the same *housing* class. Also, it seems a confusion to argue that the different housing positions of a labourer who rents his house from the council and that of a postman who owns his house in the same street is great enough for us to say that these two occupy different *class* positions.

Rex, it will be remembered, asserted that any theory of class conflict must further specify how those with a common market situation organise or fail to organise in pursuit of their interests. In the empirical situation reported in *Race, Community and Conflict*, it is suggested how the forms of local organisation and the influence or racial definitions and tensions obscured the common housing interests and housing actions of local people (Rex and Moore, 1967, ch. x; and Rex, 1968, p. 218).

Our studies suggest how in *any* inner-city situation where great diversity of interest and accessibility exists, opportunities for organisation and activity are limited. Moreover, the focus on housing as a separate and distinct set of interests with a market or markets of their own, as is implicit in the idea of *housing class*, is misleading. However, in rejecting the concept, whether as formulated by Rex or by Pahl, we would not underestimate the significance of various forms of protest, conflict and struggle over housing but would stress the need to relate them to other processes: to see, in short, housing as part of collective consumption (see pp. 15–17).

Our case studies demonstrate the difficulties that exist for locality based groups and organisations to take effective action in pursuit of their interests. Although there were elements in the local situation – a genuine diversity of interests in some places, a number of diversionary elements, like the labelling of racial minority groups and/or 'problem families' as *the* problem, in others – which militated against local organisation, it is not these to which we would draw attention. The major source of difficulty lay in the relationship between individuals and groups and officers and members of the local authority. Our case studies underline the extent to which access to housing is bureaucratically defined; hence the *political* relationship is crucial.

On the Managers

In each of the neighbourhoods studied we have been concerned with the relationship between local residents and those departments of the local authority involved with housing, planning and public health or environmental issues. In each of the areas the role of these authorities in determining the future of homes of local residents was paramount, so our neglect of other managers is not totally unreasonable. In each area the key relationship varied considerably, as did the extent of face-to-face contact between local residents and departmental officials. In each neighbourhood it was the case that local people attributed paramount influence of responsibility to the local authority; and in each neighbourhood on innumerable occasions, sometimes to an individual, sometimes to public meetings of various sizes, officers and elected members of the local authority claimed responsibility. Moreover, in claiming responsibility they claimed to be serving the interests of those to whom they spoke: as *elected* representatives or as local-government officers accountable to policy determined by elected representatives. They stressed again and again their capacity to take action. Rare were the occasions on which officers and members sought to explain or excuse what was happening in terms of their limited autonomy to act in the interests of the people who elected or employed them.

In each of our case studies the failure of the city council to maintain a high rate of council building played an important part in defining the scarcity of houses which so thwarted a clear time-tabled manageable process of environmental change. The nature of this failure is worth exploring.

Successive governments have sought to maintain and improve the output of houses in order to satisfy new demands from a rising population, to replace existing unfit housing and to cater for improved expectations. Systematically, however, there has been a failure to achieve the anticipated targets and, as a nation, Great Britain spends a smaller fraction of G. N. P. on housing than most other countries in Western Europe (U. N. Economic Commission for Europe, 1976).

However, the controls available to successive governments over the rate of output have been varied. Unlike the provision of funding for national enterprises like roads, warships, guided missiles or nuclear-power stations, the money for house-building has to be provided by the money market, both the private sector and local authorities having had to borrow in order to build. Nationally, over 70 per cent of expenditure in local-authority housing revenue accounts goes on debt charges, and of that only 30 per cent redeems the capital, the rest consists of interest. Thus about 50 per cent of local-authority housing expenditure is comprised of interest payments alone (Merrett, 1975). In Birmingham net rental income to the housing revenue account for 1972 – 3 was £20.8 million. In the same year, interest, debt repayment and debt management amounted to over £22 million (Report of Housing Committee to Birmingham City Council, October 1973). Land and the building industry remain of course in private ownership and their profitability, albeit at fluctuating levels, has been a sustained feature of recent years. This economic framework is fundamental to any discussion of the present situation.

From 1969 a downward turn in output was apparent which in 1973 and 1974 amounted to a slump. In the first part of the period the decline was greater in the public sector but, in the latter part, private house-building showed the greatest decline. Both sectors were operating during a period of rapidly rising costs, severe shortages of supplies, and difficulties of finding adequate labour.

The situation in Birmingham parallels the national situation. In 1970, 5700 council houses were completed; in 1973 the figure was 1400 and had only risen to 2360 by 1974. In the four years 1970 – 3 less than 4500 new private houses were completed, whereas in the previous four years the annual total was more than 6500.

In a report to the city council in October 1973, the housing committee took pains to explain its difficulties in terms of the following factors:

1. The Central Government ruling that all contracts of under two years duration must be on a firm basis – and contractors are

obviously reluctant to quote under these conditions during this period of escalating prices.
2. Shortage of craft labour and materials.
3. The volume of alternative work available.
4. The reluctance of contractors to tender under such conditions (Report of the Housing Committee to Birmingham City Council, October 1973).

The report also described the consequences of the government's failure to adjust the building cost yardstick which regulated council building. For almost a year the city council found that tendering was at a standstill because contractors could not operate within the yardstick limits. Only in October 1972 did the Department of the Environment adjust the yardstick which made building possible again, but it was still bound by the limitation of a two-year, 'firm-price' clause.

The two-year limitation for fixed price tenders was especially difficult for small- and medium-sized projects. Large-scale plans were relatively free from the restraint. The housing committee listed in their report the results of tenders for eighty specific schemes between May 1972 and July 1973. Only twenty-seven of the schemes obtained tenders and in only ten of these were more than one tender obtained. A list of forty-six contractors was used and each had indicated an interest in tendering for the specific size of scheme. All but six of these schemes were for small- to medium-sized house-building projects. In total the projects involved about 3000 dwellings.

One issue that the report did not touch on related to the city council's directly employed house-building force. This was started in 1954 and disbanded in the mid-1960s by the Conservative Party when in power. Steps were taken in 1972 to revive it. Clearly the plans were for the gradual development of a substantial building enterprise, and the shortage of craft labour and materials is indicative of its slow progress towards viability. With hindsight it is easy to pick on the decision to disband the force as a self-inflicted wound of some importance.

A further factor not mentioned in the report was the absence of the building firm of Bryants from the list of contractors interested in tendering. The association between the council and Bryants stretches back many years but its heyday was the late 1960s, when the firm had a virtual monopoly of success with council tenders. It became a hugely profitable enterprise with developing interests in private house-building. But in 1972 the firm withdrew from all future tendering, claiming that there was a more profitable world elsewhere, which undoubtedly there was. Subsequently the situation was plunged into the murk and chaos of a major corruption scandal, for which the city's chief architect and some private architects involved in sub-contracting work were jailed for receiving bribes. It seems likely that the domination of one firm and its withdrawal and the emergence of a corruption scandal did not enhance the city's task in attracting other firms to build their houses when other more profitable work was plentiful in the locality.

The housing committee did not explore how much of the volume of alternative work available in the Midlands to major contractors was in some way controlled or influenced by the city council. It was noticeable that major city centre building developments, mainly offices, the new public library, as well as the National Exhibition Centre, experienced little difficulty in making rapid progress. It seems that shortages of labour and materials posed no insurmountable problems in those instances.

It was not surprising, in fact, that such schemes progressed. Major contractors will work on those projects which achieve the highest rate of return. Thus new civic developments, the redevelopment of the wholesale markets (both projects funded by the public sector) and the increased scope for office building under the Conservative government ensured better profits than house-building. These developments had the effect of attracting contractors and their labour away from providing houses, as well as using up plant and materials.

There was, further, no attempt to explain or question the whole basis of the financing of house-building in the report of the housing committee. Other authorities, faced with the national context of constraints, virtually ceased to build houses. In Birmingham, however, it was clearly the task of the council to press on despite the difficulties, and to argue for a more tolerant context within which to operate. It was not a report in which one should expect to find an analysis of the *political* constraints on house-building, yet it describes very adequately how the city council was limited in its powers to alter the situation. The housing committee's plans for a major house-building scheme in North Worcestershire outside the city's boundaries had also been delayed, but for reasons other than those being discussed. In 1966 the city council had sought powers to build in North Worcestershire to overcome its land shortage and to allow continuity for the building programme following the completion of the massive Chelmsley Wood development. The government requested a report in 1967 and the fierce objections from Worcestershire, the planning authority, meant that it was not until 1971 that permission for a limited development was granted. By this time all the former causes of delay mentioned in the October 1973 report, together with continued difficulties between Birmingham and Worcestershire, were operative. No contractor could be found to start work until 1973, and the first houses did not materialise until a year later.

Faced with such difficulties in maintaining a house-building programme, what alternatives were possible, and what were the effects? Apart from pressing on with its own building attempts, the housing committee sought to launch a variety of schemes to assist first-time house purchasers with especially attractive mortgage schemes, for, while council-house-building was declining, there was not so marked a reduction in private house-building until 1973–4. There was, however, a very considerable increase in prices, in part reflecting escalating land and building costs, but also a consequence of growing scarcity aggravated by a bulge in the 26–29 age-group, a peak age for first-time buying. An indicator of this peaking was provided by the state of the housing register. Applicants continued at the fairly constant level of 8000–9000 which had been a feature of recent years. But in previous years deletions and withdrawals from the register had been at between 5000–7000, as many applicants found alternatives to council tenancies through home ownership. In 1972 and 1973, withdrawals and deletions dropped sharply to nearly 2500 as people, particularly young families who would be first-time buyers, found themselves priced out of the market.

The delay in the start of the North Worcestershire scheme is particularly relevant here. An important part of the proposed development was of houses for purchase and where council mortgages for waiting-list applicants and council tenants would be available. The delay thus contributed to the worsening situation in two ways: not only were there fewer houses to buy, but also there were more, especially young, families with children dependent upon council houses, fewer of which were becoming available for waiting-list applicants. The *Evening Mail* voiced the consequences; it ran reports of the housing committee's efforts and plans to assist waiting-list families with a series of special schemes, low-start mortgages, half-rent/half-mortgage schemes and 100 per cent loans, and a series of news stories about families having to remain with in-laws, living in cramped rooms while stuck on the waiting list.

In other cities squatting was one organised or semi-organised response to acute housing shortage. In Birmingham this has not been the case. In some London boroughs, where squatting has become virtually institutionalised, it has depended on the existence of council-owned, short-life property and on a willingness on the part of the squatters, a housing association and/or a borough council to find an alternative when the property was required. Squatting has therefore provided a means of maximum utilisation of short-life property.

In Birmingham the city council has managed properties in clearance areas and ensured swift demolition or complete dereliction immediately after the last tenants have left. The housing department's grading of some families as only suitable for sub-standard property has meant that houses which in other cities might have harboured a 'squat' have been let by the council for this category of people.

Those incidents of squatting which have occurred and attracted publicity have been unorganised and individualistic responses to seemingly hopeless housing situations. They have usually been a means of forcing pressure on the housing department. No squatting organisations have appeared in Birmingham at the time of writing.

In summary, then, the period in which we were studying found Birmingham city council unable to maintain a momentum for the progress of its plans. It lacked sufficient controls and was bound by a tendency in national housing policy which prevented its priorities setting the pace. In the face of high demand and reduced production, house prices soared. Landowners, builders and existing property owners enjoyed the benefits. The relatively unprivileged who were priced out of the market stayed within the public sector or joined the queue if they were not there already. The point to be made is that Birmingham's failure was central government success. The decline in council building was not accidental but was determined by *policy*. Birmingham sought to resist, adapt and cushion the effects but it was not master over its own priorities and policies. An even clearer example of this relates to the controversy over the 1972 Housing Finance Act, which was of course part of the same tendency in national housing policy. Just as policy on building cost yardsticks and on supervision of loan agreements, whereby local councils raise the funds to finance housing development, reflects central-government control over local authorities, subsidies are provided to encourage and enable the development. Rents paid by council tenants do not reflect the full cost but are subsidised.

The purpose of the Act was to phase out this subsidy through a series of rises to what were to be called 'fair rents'. Through a complex means-tested system of rent rebates, the effect of rises to fair rents was to be redistributed among council tenants as a whole. Subsidy report was to be phased out as rent rises improved the income of local-authority housing revenue accounts. A parallel set of 'fair rent' rises was authorised for the private unfurnished rented sector which was to be partly offset by rent allowances for those in need. Control over council rent levels was to pass from local authorities to government-appointed rent scrutiny boards. To give the Act teeth, the Secretary of State for the Environment was given powers to withdraw all subsidy, deprive local authorities of their housing powers and appoint housing commissioners to fulfil the purpose of the Act. Severe penalties on councillors and officers obstructing its implementation were also included.

The Housing Finance Act was a measure designed to discourage the growth of the council-house sector, to promote a 'property-owning democracy' and to limit the role of council housing to a welfare or 'safety-net' function. It particularly aimed at those authorities who had built large stocks of council housing for the working class. It sought to imply that council-house tenants were especially and unfairly privileged.

The public issues of the Housing Finance Act were almost entirely concerned with the proposed rent rises for council tenants. In Birmingham, despite opposition to the Act and a policy of non-implementation being important issues at the local election in May 1972 when Labour regained control of the city council, the new Labour leadership entered into negotiations with the Department of the Environment for 'nil increases' within the terms of the Act because of existing high rents, the surplus on its housing revenue account and the strong feeling that the city council should retain control over decisions affecting its housing. The Secretary of State agreed to some reduction in the proposed rent increases, partly because Birmingham had phased out rate support to the housing revenue account in 1963 and was thus already charging relatively high rents. After much delay, and on a free vote, a majority of the council agreed the Act's implementation.

The broader issues of subsidies, of the function of council housing, and of the limited way the proposed rents were 'fair', scarcely received a hearing; the apparent inconsistencies of these with other aspects of

Conservative 'housing policy were, again, not considered. Yet by and large in all of the areas we studied the implications of this policy were being felt directly.

A further aspect of national housing policy consistent with the above drive against the public sector in terms of reduced building and higher rents was the shift from large-scale clearance and rebuilding to grant-aided improvement to prevent obsolescence. Again we can observe Birmingham resisting, then following the logic of this policy, not so much out of choice but simply because there was no alternative, there being little scope to operate autonomously and devise policies in the interests of local people. This was especially the case for local people in our neighbourhoods: in the redevelopment area the houses were beyond improvement; in the action area the scope and capacity for improvement was greater but the confidence was lacking, especially because of uncertainty about the future of unimprovable houses; in the street block 'saved for improvement', few residents, without compulsion and direction, had the means or will to do it; and in the neighbourhood where our involvement was in housing advice the tendency for improvement, whether by landlords or housing associations, reduced the number of housing units available.

But, it might be argued, isn't improvement a popular alternative, isn't it 'what the people want'? Our experience is that for many it *was* what was wanted when they faced the alternative. Given the choice between a long wait in a blighted area before a move to an unspecified (of type, age, condition, price and location) council dwelling and remaining in an improved older house, then most people will prefer the improvement option. However, if redevelopment *could* mean decisive, rapid clearance, local rehousing for those who wanted it, perhaps using techniques of 'cellular renewal' or 'phasing', as it was called in one of our areas, then the prospect of a local, modern council house, even with a higher rent, meant that redevelopment was better than improvement any day.

However, it was precisely this sort of control over redevelopment which Birmingham (as with so many redeveloping authorities) lacked, for it could not control the availability of land, materials and resources to build enough houses of the right size and location to promote a 'popular' redevelopment process. Precisely the same constraints limited the capacity of the planners to respond except in a technical way to the participatory pressure in the action area. And, as we observed in our discussion of housing-allocation policies, it was not the fault of officials that they had insufficient homes to meet demands and so were obliged to sustain the apparatus of the queue to preserve order.

The issues of rates of house-building and of improvement policies show the extent to which local-authority action is limited by a complex web of forces deriving from central government and the market. Even in the case study which concentrates on local rules determining access to council and housing association housing, it is apparent that the influence of Rent Acts and planning legislation affecting multi-occupation, and of Housing Acts allowing housing association enterprises to develop further, underlines the role of local government as interpreter and agent of central power, not as creative initiator of autonomous policies and practices.

Obviously this is not peculiar to Birmingham, though there were no doubt some aspects of managerial style which were particular to the local situation. Birmingham is a large city with large centralised departments which were, at the time of our study, only just beginning to be reduced in size in part to counter criticisms of impersonality, unapproachability and poor public relations – criticisms which our studies have borne out. However, whatever the local size and style of management, it seems unlikely that it is only in Birmingham that officials and representatives like to claim responsibility and so to convey their sense of power. But whatever their claims and hopes they can only represent local interests to the extent that these government and market constraints permit. The wonder was that they were so infrequently referred to in the transactions and episodes which constituted the relationship between themselves and those whose interests and futures they managed.

The Response of 'the Managed'

Our case studies have referred to the individual and collective efforts of local residents to discover how they were situated. Much of the activity with which we were concerned in Birmingham is part of a broader phenomenon which may be termed 'community action'. At one level analysis is unproblematic: such participatory efforts are a vital part of democratic forms of government. In the 1970s the concern for participation in planning achieved statutory recognition and further legitimated a variety of local efforts in many neighbourhoods and most cities for citizens to have their say.

Our experience, however, was that, whatever the theoretical or statutory legitimacy attached to participatory efforts, the yield was remarkably slight.

This was not so much a question of the legitimacy of the participating groups, though the standing, representativeness and coherence of organisation was, as we have suggested, varied. The greater problem derived from being locality based groups in a situation in which the issues were not limited to, or determined by, the locality. The redevelopment area, for instance, was one of several in the same sort of plight in the city. However, it was by no means clear how priorities were being determined. In a real sense the different areas were in competition with each other for the same scarce resources, the too-few new houses and casual vacancies for relets which determine the actual rate of clearance. Was the aim of local action to be to claim priority status or to obtain changes in city-wide policy and practice to alleviate the situation common to all redevelopment areas?

The action area was one among a number of areas subject to such planning proposals by a small group of planners. There were other pressures on those planners from other areas; furthermore, it became apparent that decisions of priority were not determined by these planners or even by the department in which they were located. So was the purpose of participation to accept or challenge those different sorts of priority definition?

If the organised groups focused on *local* issues and claims then they found themselves confronted by officers and chairmen who would stress that in a large city it is only the authority who is in a position to judge correctly the priority to be attached to local claims. We were continually being made aware of systems of allocating priorities in which our area's and residents' needs were relatively unimportant.

To seek debate on the nature and significance of local problems was difficult. At an administrative level the existence of only city-wide departments for some services, and others organised locally, but all unco-ordinated, meant that the flow of information which would have allowed for co-ordinated assessment was well nigh impossible. At a political level the legitimate route for local issues to get an airing is through the party and party-group systems which dominate local politics. A councillor is influential not in terms of his locality connections but in terms of his standing in the party. Most of the councillors representing our areas were Labour members; after the 1972 local elections they were thus part of the majority party in the city council, one or two of them senior members of the Labour group. But they had to face the same tensions as existed for all councillors – the critical tension between responsibilities 'for the city as a whole' and to their immediate electorate.

Frequently dependent upon officers' definitions of problems and approaches to policy, councillors rarely raise local issues in public. Debate takes place within the Labour group, but the member's first loyalty is to the group not his electorate. This is the same for all major parties; public dissent is reserved for set pieces, with local members' major displays of representation consisting of little more than the presentation of petitions in the council chamber.

The effects of this professionalised and departmentalised administrative structure on the one hand, and the city-wide party political systems of policy and priority determination on the other, are acute for local groups. To become an effective pressure group, there appeared to be two sorts of choice, each of which had its own limitations and dangers.

The first choice was to be primarily a *local* group; but this tended to impose upon the group priorities and definitions of the local situation which were laid down elsewhere. For example, both in the redevelopment area and the action area the organised groups found that to lobby on the local issues – 'incidents' is perhaps a better word – they needed a line to some sympathetic or responsive official in a relevant department. In the redevelopment area almost the only result of group pressure was a series of individual favours, but there was no hint of steps being taken to prevent future recurrences of the same sort of problems. In the action area the residents' association discovered how their responsive contact with the planners was limited to technical co-operation with that department and its rules and priorities which carried no weight in other departments' problems. Both these groups found that a councillor's support was effective within narrow limits – the limits of what was expected of a local councillor in the elaborate politico-professional system of urban administration.

To become a *city-wide pressure group* posed other sorts of problems for local groups. As our study grew to a close a federation of associations in areas affected by the new policy proposals was established but has experienced the same confusion over the decisions of officers, the role of the members' committee, the location of the policy within a departmental hierarchy and the contextual web of central-government policy. Moreover, they have experienced how much of the policy is a zero-sum game in which different areas are in competition for scarce resources, and in these circumstances there is only limited purpose in co-operation because of the policy's fundamental need to ration what is scarce (Paris and Blackaby, forthcoming).

One conclusion we would draw from these diverse experiences of action and group pressure is in terms of the common difficulty of getting through to a hearing. We would not overestimate the strength and tenacity of these local groups and in our third case study we have stressed the non-emergence of a group even to begin to exert pressure. The point here is that there were groups and associations formed out of protest and discontent which were trying to press a point of view, or even to obtain a hearing from those 'in charge' about what was going on; but the structure of local government was experienced as unyield-ing, disinterested and unconcerned. For a great many participants the experience confirmed their sense of a 'them' who were in control of the processes which so affected their neighbourhoods. As time went by the claims of officials and councillors to be working in the interests of local people carried less and less weight with those who tried to articulate interests in relation to which officers and councillors might work. The relationship between urban managers and local populations and their groups is essentially a relationship of control. This control was not oppressive, overtly violent or achieved by explicit coercion; it was the more effective for being achieved through methods whereby legitimacy was accorded *them*, to do what *they* would – for that was what the system was all about.

We would draw attention to three elements in managerial style which seemed effective in achieving control over individual and group protests whereby the claim of legitimacy was advanced. Each, we would suggest, are part of the assumptions and beliefs about how 'things should be done' which are presented as part of what 'everyone knows and takes for granted'.

The first is the assertion of the *technical* nature of the problem and the special competence gained through professional training of the man-agers to deal with the problems. The common appeal that is implicitly made (and sometimes explicitly) by the managers to local people is along the following lines: 'We are trying to do something important but complicated. However, there exist a number of proven techniques and these are part of and supported by a substantive body of knowledge available to professional experts. Trust us to do the job.' Representing an issue as technical, as Dennis has reported (Dennis, 1972), effectively limits the number of those competent to discuss it. It puts ordinary people at a distance and at a disadvantage. It confronts them with the paraphenalia of the technicians – maps, plans, zonings, hatchings, symbols and formulae through which everyday issues and problems are translated for the purposes of administration. Such displays are of course part of the means whereby the competence of these technicians is asserted. When 'participation' is offered within this context, it invariably involves explaining the present situation in administrative and technical terms which bar certain areas from questioning. As the residents' association in the action area found, 'technical co-operation' was time-consuming, engaging but ultimately a limiting experience; it did not lead to any co-operation over those issues and concerns which were central to the residents' interests.

The second aspect of managerial style or ideology we would stress as significant relates to its concern for individual need and service. Problems of material shortage or of neighbourhood decline were treated as one of individual need to be satisfied by the personal attention and service of the official concerned. Housing officials would stress how each case was treated on its merits, appearing chary about asserting the influence of general rules; at public meetings officials and councillors were happiest when able to respond to individual complaints by taking a name and address and promising a special 'look into' the matter. The rules of meetings seemed to be that an *individual* case could not be discussed in public and general problems were reinterpreted to become the questioner's private concern (or individual case), or else something not really that person's private concern, so perhaps none of his business. Only the organised resident's council in the action area succeeded in breaking down this pattern at public meetings by insisting on general policy discussion – but those meetings typically declined into a discussion of solely individual concerns; and because each was treated with the familiar tone of 'leave your name, we'll investigate it specially', each such question provoked further individual questions and ensured queues at the end of each meeting of those waiting to give their name to an official or councillor. The emphasis on the special features of individual cases, the hopes raised by the prospect of discretionary treatment, confirmed for most residents that it was these people – officials and managers – who personally decided what happened and who got what and when. The purpose and effect of management was to underline the *dependency* of people; there was little sign of their treatment as citizens with equal rights in relation to declared policies. Councillors and officers presented themselves as persons from whom favours could be sought. Even in terms of scarcity and shortage, though overworked and hard-pressed by many claims, they would do their best to see if something could be done; special attention was given, special visits were made, exceptions were made and people were made offers despite the 'rules'. Perhaps the process can be best summarised by saying that management treated people as *clients*, not in the sense that a lawyer or architect employs that word, but in the sense that is used in social work.

The third element we would point to is the nature of the partnership between elected members and paid officers which characterises urban administration. The insistence by both officers and councillors on the scope for discretionary decisions for individuals makes the nature of policy in its local effects hard to discern. The dividing-line between what officers did as a result of decisions by elected members in committee and what was implementation, interpretation and dis-cretion was far from clear. The role of the local councillor seemed to consist in hearing out individual complaints and communicating them to a senior officer with a request for investigation. The councillors in our areas did not typically display any deep knowledge or interest in the processes at work in the neighbourhoods. The housing department contained a small specialised section which dealt almost exclusively with councillors' requests which appeared to limit effectively the amount of direct influence or access councillors had to officials unless they were part of some committee or sub-committee. Officers tended to imply that councillors and their enquiries were something that had to be put up with but policy was something quite different. Policy seemed to be much more a set of established customs, past decisions and agreed practices which governed what was to be done; officers and councillors adhered to it and its legitimacy stemmed from this agreement. Discretion in individual cases was possible without damaging broad lines of policy and individual and group requests and the response of councillors and officials were to be seen in that context.

The effects of managerial style containing these three interlinked themes or aspects can be suggested in relation to what Howard Becker has termed an 'hierarchy of credibility':

In a system of ranked groups, participants take it as given that members of the highest group have the right to define the way things really are . . . from the point of view of a well socialized participant in the system; any tale told by those at the top intrinsically deserves to be regarded as the most credible account obtainable of the organisation's working (by analogy, the same argument holds for the social classes of a community) (Becker, 1971b, pp. 126–7).

An acceptance of the dominant accounts of what could be achieved by planners and of what was fair and proper in matters of housing allocation was common among those residents with whom we worked. The terms of debate and discussion were set by those who managed resource allocation; such debate and discussion as there was related to varieties of individual need, on the discretion to allocate existing resources in slightly different ways, not about the adequacy of the resources, the source of the resources or of alternatives. The consequence of this intervention is to make relatively deprived people apparently patient acceptors of the existing pattern of resource allocation: crucially, what is obscured by these presentations of urban management is the selective and systematic pattern of deprivation which is sustained. In that respect, these aspects of managerial style can be said to be 'ideological'. They contain assumptions and explanations which draw attention to some features and conceal others. The effects, as we have observed, tend to set queueing individual against queueing individual, neighbourhood against neighbourhood and exaggerate the capacity of the local-authority apparatus to respond to pressures 'from below', while obscuring the processes which sustain profit, scarcity, and territorial and individual inequality.

The Role of the State in Urban Management

Our study concentrated on the relationship between residents in inner-city neighbourhoods and officials and members of the local authority. The managerial style we have depicted effectively controls protest about existing conditions. Broadly, the promise was 'wait and you will get your reward'. For the impatient and the sceptical, there was always the record, the achievement to be referred to – acre after acre of modern council-built suburbia, houses and flats, low and high rise, a direct reflection of the capacity of Birmingham city council to put the interests of the city's working class to the forefront of its priorities. The recently published official history of the city has drawn attention to it as 'a community in which personal success and contentment were so widely distributed' that 'a voluble political life was unlikely'. 'The calm state of Birmingham politics,' it remarks, 'was largely the product of the

City's prosperous economy and generally good environment.' For most citizens, they argue, there was an over-all confidence in their city council to maintain the quality of life (Sutcliffe and Smith, 1974, p. 477). Certainly 'civic pride' flourishes in the city and the spirit of Joseph Chamberlain is still a powerful presence. Birmingham is the largest single local authority in Britain and has maintained a highly centralised structure to its organisation and administration. Power is concentrated and valued, but the limitations and constraints on that power are rarely explicated.

We would argue that the form of city government has a strong influence on the sort of local protests and organisations (to get things changed, or improved, or simply just done) which arise. The ideology of civic responsibility for public issues like housing is a marked feature of local government. As the largest local authority, and consistent with its motto 'Forward', the council seeks to provide the leadership and resources for most endeavours. There has often been considerable unanimity within the council, irrespective of political party, about important areas of public policy. A primary sphere of policy has been in relation to housing and planning, in particular the physical lay-out and renewal of the city. The road system and housing provision are the city council's special pride. In contrast to the national reputation gained by Birmingham in the sphere of house- and road-building, the more directly 'person-centred' services, education and social services, have tended to attract little by way of reputation outside of the city. But in bricks and mortar matters, in homes and roads, nobody surpasses Birmingham city council, and it seems that there is little it can learn from elsewhere. This caricature of a complex set of ideas and values is, none the less, an important part of the council's relations to other bodies.

While we believe that Sutcliffe and Smith tend to overstate the equanimity, that indeed there are and always have been profound party-political differences, that varying relationships between local and central government have been important in determining policy, none the less the 'official face' remains surprisingly unchanged. In the face of criticism, from whatever direction, the claims of municipal competence persist.

We would suggest that the managerial style we have depicted (and the extremely limited scope for participation) is consistent with that claim. We would further suggest that the calm and passivity of local politics reflects the form of control maintained by the politico-technical partnership that is the local authority over the terms and content of political debate. The question to be asked is in whose interest is this control and competence exerted. In the pluralist conception of the state, elected representative government prevents the domination of any one interest while ensuring the articulation of many. Within this kind of framework rests Castells's view of town planning's claims 'to resolve insurmountable difficulties, to get round the conflicts, and to put an end to disputes in the name of a technical rationality by means of which divergent social interests can be reconciled' (Castells, 1973). On the face of it Birmingham would seem to have fulfilled that claim by dint of its formidable local apparatus of urban management.

Our case studies have demonstrated that whatever the claim and whatever the achievement, for many of those living in the neighbourhoods what was occurring did not feel like a reconciliation, rather it was experienced as control. Efforts at participation led not to acknowledgement and recognition but to negation. Not only was no notice taken, but no change occurred. With reference to house-building and other aspects of housing policy, we have suggested how Birmingham city council was partially controlled by central-government dictates; moreover, we sought to show how those dictates appeared in no way to reflect the interests and claims of local residents.

So what kind of gain for working-class interests has been the achievement of council housing in Birmingham and how should we explain after fifty years of state involvement continuing scarcity, hardship and relative poor standards for a substantial sector of the city's working class. And if that has been a gain, at whose expense?

It would take a very different sort of study than that undertaken here to measure the full economic effects of council-house provision on different groups. But there are a number of points to be made.

First, the purposes of state housing policy in Britain since the period of the First World War has been to ensure production of sufficient homes at rent levels within reach of workers' wages. The political demand for this provision has been a major feature of social-policy debate. Such provision is not merely a working-class demand, it is also essential for the reproduction of the work-force; workers housed conveniently for the work-place, and at rents which do not make demands on wages, also satisfy the interests of employers. And as industrial development has become more centralised and more a mass and routine process, so the needs of the work-force for housing has grown. The fusion of the demands of the working class with the interests of capital (the owners of industry) means that the provision of housing is both unprofitable for capital and a matter of politics – hence a matter of state provision.

In Britain this provision, while being an unprofitable part of capitalist enterprise (money put into housing as investment is a low-return/high-risk investment), was none the less still linked to private investment. The risk of investment was taken over, but not the ownership of land, nor the building and construction industries, nor the source of financing for housing development. The local state housing enterprise borrows money at market rates with which it compensates landowners, provides profitable work for the privately owned building industry and charges rents which are needed to cover these costs and which have risen as those costs – other people's profits – have risen. The *production* of workers' housing continues to be predominantly the task of private enterprise, but now the customer is the local state rather than a private landlord. The owners of capital and land, and the privately owned building industry, reap the profits. In this sense, the position of the council tenant is little different from that of the tenant of large private landlords. This elementary sketch of a complex process serves to stress that whatever 'gain' is represented by council housing for the working class, such provision has also provided gain and profit for the owners of capital, i.e. the task of the state has been to reconcile different interests, absorb the risk, safeguard private profit and deflect protest.

Second, we should note that the provision has not only been inadequate in terms of quantity, but has often been of a type and style which reflects more the needs of the producers than the desires of the consumers. In Birmingham, as in many cities, for years the typical product was a high-rise block conceived with little regard for future occupiers but believed by producers to be a cost-effective means of achieving high output. By 1973, in this city whose council housing is presented as an achievement, we heard officers and councillors *warn* audiences of tenants and owners of old houses in the city's inner and middle rings that if they failed to improve their houses a flat in a high-rise block on a suburban estate might be their housing future. As we have shown, the complex and authoritarian mode of allocation which supports this state provision is a direct reflection both of its great diversity in quality, in the way people's housing aspirations in style and location do not fit with what has been provided, and also of its over-all and continuing scarcity.

So the kind of gain represented is of a complex and ambiguous kind.

This demonstrates the validity of Castells's point that it is at best a *partial* wresting from the bourgeoisie that the working class has achieved in relation to housing provision. It is not at the expense of the ruling or dominant class that this provision has been made. Profit for housing remains real and substantial; by and large middle-class owners do not queue for their homes, experience authoritarian allocation systems, have to make do with uncongenial housing types, or, despite subsidies, pay as much for their better housing as those whose earnings and prospects make them dependent upon the public sector. The idea of the privileged council tenant cushioned by subsidy and security in ideal housing conditions simply does not bear scrutiny. There are some excellent council houses let at reasonable rents to fortunate individuals: but the dominant features of life in the public sector, or awaiting entry into it, are quite a different story. Together with the myth of the privileged council tenant, so also collapses the myth of the pluralist state as neutral arbiter preventing the domination of one class, as well as the claim of town planning to reconcile divergent interests.

For Rex, in his formulation of housing classes, a system of class conflict can be modified into one of status rankings when mobility between ranks is possible and the system achieves legitimacy (Rex, 1968). Miliband, on the other hand, argues that there are diverse and elaborate processes of legitimation which continually stress the possibility of change within the existing order, the scope for accessibility and mobility; such processes mask the essential class nature of such societies whereby systematic inequalities and continued domination of some interests persist (Miliband, 1973). The very complexity of various alternative and complementary state policies towards housing, changing both geographically and over time, further distorts the broad structure of class relations. State intervention systematically fragments rather than unifies class interests; to that extent separate *housing* classes might have some meaning. But this structure, which is the product of state policies, can also be changed by state policy, and should not be confused with class differences based on wealth, property and power.

Therein lies, we suggest, the most significant effect of the current mode of urban managerialism as depicted in our case studies on housing and planning issues in Birmingham. The effect of management was to establish and sustain the present mode of provision by controlling allocation through systems of grading, of queueing and of presenting scarcity as an inevitable part of the economic order. By asserting their autonomy, local managers prescribed themselves as the legitimate source of what was needed. Time and again, whether waiting for a decent house or experiencing the agonisingly slow chaos of redevelopment, or negotiating with planners, or being told of the novel status of G. I. A. for their neighbourhood, the relative sense of dependency among local residents upon a large and powerful technocracy was underlined.

We have stressed how management style underscores individual needs as against collective rights. Councillors, managers and advisers, in explaining the present system of resource allocation, had to admit scarcity and the extraordinary difficulties of discrimination among diverse and pressing forms of individual need. Most people accepted the presented notions of fairness and need without argument, though their experience was that things were not fair; but they accepted the authoritative assertion of fairness, the panoply of need, priority, problem and technicality which was the proffered explanation of things as they are. Most people kept back their bitterness and argument for private discussions or for a ceremonial outburst at a public meeting. There seemed to be no way in which their interests were articulated except through the antiseptic filter of local government. Local-authority officers would listen, explain and perhaps look for an individual remedy and favour. Most of the elected representatives knew little of the detail and the process of policy administration; they accepted much as unchangeable and inevitable, though they, too, on occasions, could perform individual favours. For most people argument, opposition and protest were unfamiliar, rather frightening forms of behaviour with unknown consequences. A subordinated value system which makes what 'they' say credible and powerful was being constantly reinforced.

So we see the *style* of urban managerialism as having potent ideological force in shaping and reinforcing the dominant pattern of power, influence and profit. Its style obscured the systematic nature of inequality and deprivation. Its tendency for competency and technicality, its claim of power and responsibility, were mystifications. An important feature of this style was that it involved locally elected representatives and publicly accountable local-government officers in partnership. It is not an overtly repressive mode of management, but one which maintained systematic inequalities. Its ability to control the terms, the forms and the content of local political debate and action removed from local politics important issues about the unequal distribution of scarce resources and successfully redefined public issues as private troubles and political issues are technical concerns. In so doing those agencies involved in urban management inhibited forms of collective action, influenced forms of collective consciousness and thereby performed in this realm of their work one of the classic functions of the state: that of managing the interests of the ruling class.

But a Marxist analysis of the state, as Lojkine argues, goes further than this: 'The bourgeois State has a dual function: (i) to maintain the cohesion of the social foundation as a whole; (ii) to directly enforce the domination of the bourgeoisie' (Lojkine, 1976).

In the provision of the means of collective consumption lies the means of achieving these apparently contradictory functions of cohesion and domination. We would suggest that our case studies reveal part of the means whereby the contradiction is resolved; for managerial style is not simply repressive and coercive, but a mixture of toleration, flexibility, seeming generosity, participation and opportunity – but ultimately controlling in its insistence on individual dependency. The other feature we would stress is its routine and everyday character. What we have described in this study are not exceptional struggles and conflicts, fiercely fought campaigns, nor large and highly publicised issues. We believe that in many neighbourhoods of many cities for many a year similar stories could be told. The power of capital, Westergaard and Resler remind us:

> is revealed much less in positive acts of decision-making – involving conflict and choice between alternative policies – than in the everyday, for much of the time unquestioned, application of those assumptions which give priority to private capital accumulation and market exchange in the use and distribution of resources. Power is to be found more in uneventful routine than in conscious and active exercise of will (Westergaard and Resler, 1976, p. 144).

That kind of power and the associated powerlessness of the majority of citizens are revealed in the relations between the managerial representatives of the state and local residents over the issues of housing and planning which have been the concern of this study.

Concluding Note

It had originally been our intention to conclude with an outline of an alternative approach to housing policy. Many readers may feel that we should tackle such questions as 'how, as the best homes are always in short supply, can allocation be most fairly determined?' But that is to miss the most fundamental point of all: *we do not take for granted that shortage and inequality are inevitable* – there are many residential districts in Birmingham and elsewhere that are *not* overcrowded, dirty, poorly serviced, etc. Many of our citizens have two or more cars, two or more houses even; still a minority of the population owns most of the wealth, receives most of the income, has most control of the economy.

These are issues which cannot be divorced from the insecurity, poverty and powerlessness of the people with whom we worked. They are parts of the same process, located within the same social formation.

We do not want the reader to conclude that somehow 'the local authority' or 'the government' is the culprit. Of course, both operate under tremendous constraints; that, too, is fundamental to our analysis. The critical issue, though, is the extent to which these constraints are articulated, made the subject for debate, and the routine ways in which differential ability to influence the future are accomplished.

We have always sought to address our work to theoretical issues, deriving from recent literature in urban sociology. Our initial concerns with 'housing class' and 'the urban managers' were incorporated into our research programme and we have been concerned to reject the former notion and substantially redefine the latter. The learning process through which we have come to this position has been largely influenced by those theorists who have urged a critical perspective on the state itself, and on the processes whereby state policies fragment working-class interests, and state bureaucracies (at central and local levels) perform crucial ideological functions. But we are certainly not seeking to present a 'final analysis'. Since the particular work on this project has finished, we have been involved in other activities of research and action – work on other policies, other processes of interaction, and involvement in political practice.

In many ways, of course, our studies have been about Birmingham, and in that sense our findings remain unique. To concentrate on the special features of one city, however, is to fail to grasp the importance of *locating* general theories about our society in actual empirical examples. In other cities the details of the story would undoubtedly have been different, but the general features of process and relationship would be the same. An understanding of working-class housing must be structured in terms of the dominant relationships of access, control and allocation.

Bibliography

HOWARD BECKER (1971a) 'Inference and Proof in Participant Observation', *Sociological Work*, ch. 2 (London: Allen Lane, The Penguin
Press).

HOWARD BECKER (1971b) 'Whose Side Are We On?', *Sociological Work*,
ch. 8 (London: Allen Lane, The Penguin Press).

PETER L. BERGER and THOMAS LUCKMANN (1967) *The Social Construction of
Reality* (London: Allen Lane, The Penguin Press).

ERNEST W. BURGESS (1925) 'The Growth of the City: an Introduction to a
Research Project', in *The City*, ed. Robert Park *et al.* (University of
Chicago Press).

ASA BRIGGS (1952) *History of Birmingham, Vol. II* (Oxford University
Press).

ASA BRIGGS (1963) *Victorian Cities* (Harmondsworth: Penguin).

MANUEL CASTELLS (1968) 'Y a-t-il une sociologie urbaine?', *Sociologie du
Travail*, 1; trans. in *Urban Sociology* ed. C. G. Pickvance (London:
Tavistock, 1976) pp. 33–59.

MANUEL CASTELLS (1969) 'Théorie et idéologie en sociologie urbaine',
Sociologie et Sociétés, 1; trans. in *Urban Sociology*, ed. C. G. Pickvance
(London: Tavistock, 1976) pp. 60–84.

MANUEL CASTELLS (1970) 'Propositions théoriques pour une recherche
expérimentale sur les mouvements sociaux urbains' (unpublished
paper presented at the Seventh World Congress of Sociology, Varna,
1970); trans. in *Urban Sociology*, ed. C. G. Pickvance (London:
Tavistock, 1976) pp. 147–73.

MANUEL CASTELLS (1973) *Luttes urbaines et pouvoir politique* (Paris:
Maspero) trans. as *Urban Struggles and Political Parties* by B. Lynne
Lord, mimeographed, 1973.

AARON CICOUREL (1964) *Method and Measurement in Sociology* (New
York: The Free Press).

JON GOWER DAVIES (1972) *The Evangelistic Bureaucrat* (London: Tavistock).

NORMAN DENNIS (1972) *Public Participation and Planners' Blight* (London: Faber & Faber).

RUTH GLASS (1955) 'Urban Sociology in Great Britain', *Current Sociology*, IV (4); reprinted in *Readings in Urban Sociology*, ed. R. E. Pahl (Oxford: Pergamon, 1968).

ROY HADDON (1970) 'The Location of West Indians in the London Housing Market', *New Atlantis*, 1, 2.

M. HARLOE *et al.* (1975) 'Position Paper', *Proceedings of the Conference on Urban Change and Conflict*, Centre for Environmental Studies Conference Paper 14, London.

DAVID HARVEY (1973) *Social Justice in the City* (London: Edward Arnold).

S. M. LIPSET (1963) *Political Man: the Social Bases of Politics* (New York: Doubleday).

JEAN LOJKINE (1972) 'Contribution à une théorie marxiste de l'urbanisation capitaliste', *Cahiers Internationaux de Sociologie*, 52; trans. in *Urban Sociology*, ed. C. G. Pickvance (London: Tavistock, 1976) pp. 119–46.

J. L. MACMORRAN (1973) *Municipal Public Works and Planning in Birmingham, 1852–1972* (City of Birmingham).

S. MERRETT (1975) 'Council Rents and British Capitalism', in *Political Economy and the Housing Question*, Papers presented at the Housing Workshop of the Conference of Socialist Economists, London.

RALPH MILIBAND (1973) *The State in Capitalist Society* (London: Quartet).

PETER NORMAN (1975) 'Managerialism: Review of Recent Work', in *Proceedings of the Conference on Urban Change and Conflict*, ed. M. Harloe Centre for Environmental Studies Conference Paper 14, London.

R. E. PAHL (1965) *Urbs in Rure: the Metropolitan Fringe in Hertfordshire*, London School of Economics, Geographical Papers No. 2.

R. E. PAHL (1968) 'The Rural–Urban Continuum', in *Readings in Urban Sociology*, ed. R. E. Pahl (Oxford: Pergamon Press).

R. E. PAHL (1969) 'Urban Social Theory and Research', *Working Paper No. 5*, Centre for Environmental Studies, London; reprinted in R. E. Pahl *Whose City?* (London: Longmans, 1970).

R. E. PAHL (1975) '"Urban Managerialism" Reconsidered', in *Whose City?*, rev. edn, ch. 13 (Harmondsworth: Penguin 1975).

R. E. PAHL and J. T. WINKLER (1974a) 'Economic Elites: Theory and Practice', in *Elites and Power*, ed. P. Stanworth and A. Giddens

(Cambridge University Press).

R. E. PAHL and J. T. WINKLER (1974b) 'The New Corporatism', *New Society*, 10 October, pp. 72-6.

C. PARIS and B. BLACKABY (1973) 'Research Directions in Urban Sociology, Neighbourhood Associations and Housing Oppor- tunities', *Working Paper 16*, Centre for Urban and Regional Studies, University of Birmingham.

C. PARIS and B. BLACKABY (forthcoming) 'Urban Renewal: Policy and Practice in Birmingham'.

ROBERT PARK *et al.* (1925) *The City* (University of Chicago Press); rev., edn, ed. M. Janowitz (1967).

TALCOTT PARSONS (1964) 'Communism and the West. The Sociology of the Conflict', in *Social Change*, ed. A. and E. Etzioni (New York: The Free Press).

C. G. PICKVANCE (1975a) 'On the Study of Urban Social Movements', *Sociological Review*, vol. 23; and in *Urban Sociology*, ed. C. G. Pickvance (London: Tavistock, 1976) pp. 198-218.

C. G. PICKVANCE (1975b) 'From Social Base to Social Force: Some Analytic Issues in the Study of Urban Conflict', in *Proceedings of the Conference on Urban Change and Conflict*, ed. M. Harloe, Centre for Environmental Studies Conference Paper 14, London.

C. G. PICKVANCE (ed.) (1976) *Urban Sociology* (London: Tavistock).

A. RAPOPORT (1970) 'Action Research', Paper presented to the S.S.R.C. Conference on Action Research, University of York.

LEONARD REISSMAN (1964) *The Urban Process* (New York: The Free Press).

JOHN REX and ROBERT MOORE (1967) *Race, Community and Conflict* (Oxford University Press for the Institute of Race Relations).

JOHN REX (1968) 'The Sociology of the Zone of Transition', in *Readings in Urban Sociology* ed. R. E. Pahl (Oxford: Pergamon) pp. 211-31.

DAVID SILVERMAN (1970) *The Theory of Organisations* (London: Heinemann) ch. 6 'The Action Frame of Reference'.

MARGARET STACEY (1969) *Methods of Social Research* (Oxford: Pergamon).

A. SUTCLIFFE and R. SMITH (1974) *Birmingham 1939-1970* (Oxford University Press).

UNITED NATIONS DEPARTMENT OF ECONOMIC AND SOCIAL AFFAIRS *World Housing Survey, 1974* (New York: United Nations).

JOHN WESTERGAARD and HENRIETTA RESLER (1976) *Class in a Capitalist Society* (Harmondsworth: Penguin).

LOUIS WIRTH (1938) 'Urbanism as a Way of Life', *American Journal of Sociology*, XLIV; reprinted in *Louis Wirth on Cities and Social Life*, ed. A. J. Reiss Jr. (University of Chicago Press, 1964).

Index